Popular Arts of the First World War

POPULAR ARTS
of the
FIRST WORLD WAR

Barbara Jones & Bill Howell

McGraw-Hill Book Company
New York: St. Louis: San Francisco

To the unknown soldiers, sailors and airmen, artists, designers and factory workers, wives, sweethearts and mums, who dreamed up and made the hundreds of objects in this book which bear no signature.

Frontispiece
Top left: tin-plate souvenir. *Top right:* a Parian china bust of King Albert of the Belgians; a fund raising Red Cross with Allied ribbons; and a German jack-in-the-box with Imperial Eagle and the Kaiser. It is inscribed *Dicke Berthe,* or Thick Bertha, which the Allies changed to Big Bertha. *Bottom left:* a typical cover of *La Baïonnette,* the French satirical paper. *Bottom right:* modern plastic soldiers; a pretty wooden box in the form of a shell with Allied flags; and a curious brass mug made from bullets and the base of a shell. *Down the centre:* a Red Cross postcard; Kings, Queens and Knaves from a British pack of cards; and a French handkerchief with the Russians shown as a red flag with URSS embroidered on. *Across the centre:* flag-wagging in woolwork.

Designed by Barbara Jones and Bill Howell
©1972 Barbara Jones and Bill Howell
First published in the United States by
McGraw-Hill Book Company, a subsidiary
of McGraw-Hill, Inc., 1972
SBN: 07-033006-9
Library of Congress Catalog Card Number: 72-1576
First Edition
Printed and Bound in Great Britain

FALL IN!

INTRODUCTION

This book is about the popular arts of the First World War. It is about the things that the ordinary people who were involved made for themselves or that were made in their taste; it is not concerned with the big guns and tanks in the museums, but with the little guns and tanks made cosily in wood and brass for the mantelshelf; not with the canvases of the official war artists, but with the embroidered postcards sent home from the front.

The vast majority of those who fought were not professionals, who see war as a way of life; they went through it all as civilians, caught up, and they took with them to the battlefields the habits and tastes of home.

The First World War came after a century of factory production. Until the Industrial Revolution, the poor had few things to cheer up their houses except the things they made themselves (true, there were markets, fairs and pedlars, but what they sold was mostly for personal adornment). From early in the Industrial Revolution, its products began to reach the houses of the less privileged—everything from china ornaments to picture postcards. The desire to clutter the home with objects kept pace with the flood of cheap things from the factories. These were supplemented by the things people made in the long winter evenings, and hobbies now had the new images of an industrial age to draw on for source materials. These industrial products and hand-made objects add up to popular art. It is not folk art, which is peasant and pre-industrial, and it is not fine art. Nor is it pop art, in which professional artists reinterpret the popular arts. It is certainly not kitsch, which is bourgeois and which involves a degree of cultural pretension foreign to the popular arts; to regard popular art as kitsch is artistic snobbery.

All through the nineteenth century the new middle classes emulated the rich by acquiring possessions, and by 1914 the working classes were catching up; it was an age for THINGS, for having a lot (just like now).

The influence of the Arts and Crafts movement and of Japanese art in the last years of the nineteenth century had been towards simplicity in both objects and homes, but they were minority high-brow cults, and popular taste took little notice. In any case after the turn of the century a new wave of elaboration had swept into the parlours of Europe, and everyone adored it.

The men who went from these parlours to become the armies produced, for the first and last time we know of, a great outburst of military popular art. The armies of earlier wars have left little evidence of how they spent such free time as they had. Their wars were, on the whole, less static, the maintenance of their uniforms and gear took a long time, and they usually had to do their own catering, even being left to get the raw materials by fair means or foul. The best-known handicrafts from an earlier war are the lovely boxes, carvings and ship-models made in straw, bone or feathers by French prisoners in the Napoleonic wars. Otherwise soldiers did not get down to serious artwork before 1914, but after that, in the trenches, hospitals and prison camps, bored and frustrated men, taken from their trades, sat down and fiddled with used shell cases and bully-beef tins, making and decorating things to pass the time. These objects reflected the war as they wanted (as the only way they dared) to see it. It was a decorative and decorated war; little brass aeroplanes made of cartridges, with arabesques incised on their wings; tanks made of wood with flower designs inlaid in brass.

These are visual creations, so this is a picture book. In the text we have filled in a little of the background and described some of the phenomena which provided sources for popular interpretation. The material has been grouped into chapters based on various aspects of the war. It would have been possible, of course, to have divided it according to materials used or according to whether things were manufactured or hand-made, into the broad groupings of graphics and solid objects, or the countries the things came from, or chronology or A to Z. The grouping we have chosen highlights the themes that inspired the popular arts during the years of the Great War, as most people called it at the time.

Left: knife, made from a lump of shrapnel; most such knives were made for opening letters, but this sinister looking one was used as a trench knife throughout the Spanish Civil war by a British volunteer.
Opposite: (1) Brass biplane with fuselage made from a rifle cartridge; wings have repoussé decoration of marguerites, and Maltese crosses made of copper. Presumed German. (2) Model of British service cap made from the base of a shell-case, with added brass and aluminium trim and stippled decoration. Model hats ranged from huge ones made from howitzer shells to tiny ones based on coins. (3) Brass model of tank; British. (4) British-made submarine model celebrating the Royal Navy's capture of the German UC5. (5) Zeppelin brooch made from aluminium salvaged from the wreckage. (6) Two Sheffield spoons with stippled decoration of German crosses and Imperial Crowns, one marked Charmes, the other Rambleville. Charmes and Rambervillers, near Epinal, were behind the French lines in 1918. Presumably an Allied issue decorated by a German prisoner. (7) Stippled decoration from another brass hat, made to be used as a tobacco tin.

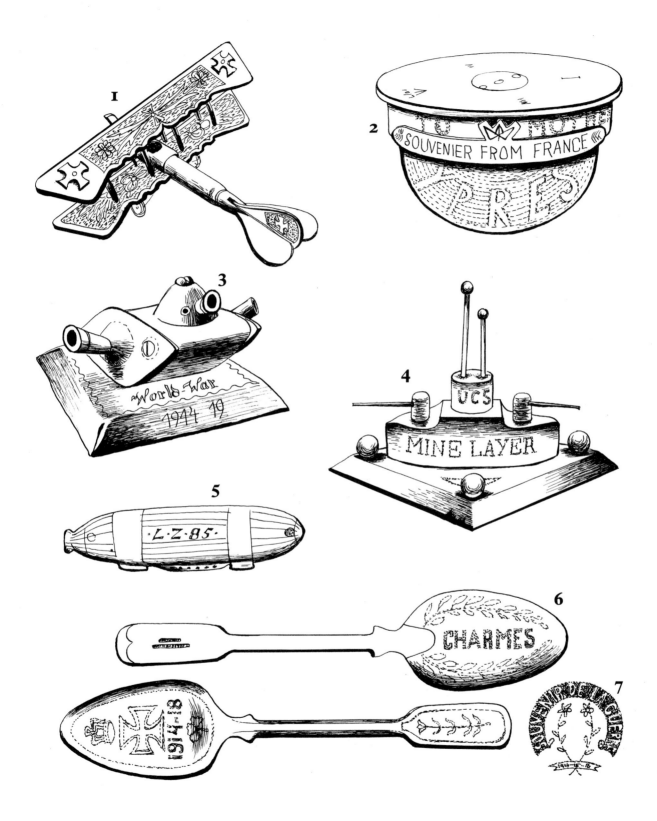

We have included as many things as possible from all countries involved but have found little except graphics from the Central Powers; they lost the war, and losers are not keepers—you don't keep souvenirs of something you'd rather forget. As in other European countries, much that was saved from the First World War went for salvage in the Second. Perhaps, too, the Germans were on a more serious war footing than their enemies, with little spare capacity for making frivolities; as we were told in Berlin, 'Maybe German soldiers found something more useful to do in their spare time. Perhaps they made something to help the war.'

Most of the things shown carry no date—even the country of origin is occasionally uncertain—and with some things it is hard to be sure that they fall precisely within the war years. Such objects do not yet have the particulars and provenance of works of fine art, and carbon dating cannot help.

We have omitted some of the most famous images of the war—Kitchener's face and that pointing finger (and the Uncle Sam equivalents), Old Bill's 'better 'ole', *Daddy, what did YOU do in the Great War?* and *Women of Britain say 'Go!'*; from France *On les Aura!* and from Germany Hindenburg's granite profile; they have been reproduced hundreds of times.

We have, however, included some examples of work by professional painters which hit the popular mood, being still firmly in the nineteenth-century tradition that every picture should tell a story, *When did you last see your father?* and *The last day in the old home.* There were, after all, plenty of stirring new stories to tell.

Top: weapons of war made small and pretty for female wear; the outer ones are amateur brasswork, the centre one the work of a professional in blue enamel. *Centre:* use, beauty and patriotism combine in this Iron Cross tea-cup. *Bottom:* souvenir hats; back row, a German pocket inkwell (kid-covered) and a French inkwell and powder box; front row, German lucky charm and assorted Allied hats made in lead (French).

The archetypal popular art form is that of the postcard. Cards were widely manufactured, turned out in millions everywhere. By 1914 the golden age of inventive design, fine printing and gay surrealism was almost over, but the war, though it gradually put a stop to the fine printing, also put new life into the designers, and some of the cards were as good as the finest of previous years. Most of these are French, a few Italian; in Germany, where in the pre-war years more than 9,000,000 cards were printed every month, the standard in design fell in postcards while it rose in posters. British wartime cards, especially the comics, were often brilliantly inventive, but printing techniques remained high only in France.

Late in the nineteenth century, a collecting craze began in Britain for small glazed white china models called Heraldic Ware or Crested China. They were mostly made in the Staffordshire potteries and are now commonly known as Crest. The pieces carried the coloured coats of arms of the resorts or towns where they were sold. There were models of local antiquities (Roman urns, Saxon beakers, etc.), buildings, busts of famous people, and thousands of universal images of holiday-making—bathing huts and bathing beauties, banjos, tennis racquets, donkeys, even Cornish pasties and beer bottles. The doyen of the industry was W. H. Goss, whose taste in subjects was more refined and scholarly (less pop) than that of his rivals, and whose products now rate higher as collectors' items. Crest was imitated abroad, especially in Germany, for export to Britain. Crest was a curious artistic convention, and the results are often comical; some things aren't easily

Top: 'Troupes Ecossaises Revenant du Combat' by François Flameng; a nice example of professional painting that must have epitomized popular taste. *Bottom:* one of the most famous paintings of the war, Matania's 'Good Bye, Old Man'; the horse has been given the last drop of water, shells are falling and an officer is calling the artilleryman urgently on (for more of Man's Best Friend, see page 149).

A piece of crested heraldic souvenir china, such as was made in dozens of factories in Britain, most of them in the Staffordshire potteries. They made hundreds of different models, each carrying the crest of the town in which it was sold. This armoured car is an odd looking vehicle; but take a look at the pictures of some of the real ones on page 68.

rendered in china, and few look natural with a municipal crest slapped on them—certainly not the female figure. The war was a great stimulus to the Crest makers, and they poured out soldiers, guns, ships, aircraft and tanks. Goss had died in 1906, and by 1914 his firm seems to have lost heart; it only made half a dozen new models based on military subjects, but its competitors made hundreds, which add up to a remarkable popular vision of the war. (The industry flourished after 1918, and made some superb Twenties cars and charabancs; it died during the depression years, when the working classes could no longer afford holidays.)

Most Great War posters were professional work; some were by amateurs and look it— the impact and simplicity needed for a successful poster were quite beyond all but a few of them. Maurice Rickards has written excellently about the posters and the war museums have collections of them, so we have shown few. We will only say that posters generally, like the bulk of Great War professional graphics, were much worse in Britain and North America than anywhere else. In Europe, especially in Germany, there was a new style of great simplicity, derived from pioneers like the Beggarstaff Brothers and leading on to the Bauhaus; it changed post-war graphics completely. The famous British image of Kitchener is certainly bold and simple enough, but the style is old-fashioned and spiritless, the last decadence of a long tradition.

The graphics in British periodicals were even worse. *John Bull*, though second to none as a poisonous hate machine, depended for its success mainly on words. However, catharsis by the comical is important in times of stress, and the dim drawings in *Punch* were no doubt helpful to many. Some of the jokes are still funny, the irony still clear, but for us who know more of the truth about casualties and 'victories' than was allowed past the rigid censorship, it is pitiful to see what ignorant little jokes kept up morale.

Posters were used in every country engaged in the war, to exhort the populace to join the forces, save food, buy war bonds and hate the enemy. This Brazilian one warned against spies and careless talk. The latter theme became a staple of poster campaigns in the Second World War, when the myth of the enemy dressed as priests also reappeared. German spies were always depicted wearing spectacles.

Opposite: one of W. Heath Robinson's amiable cartoons poking fun at German militarism from his *Some Frightful War Pictures.* The Kaiser had promised Frightfulness, but in these pictures his troops seldom did anything worse than unleash hair-restorer bombs to tie up their enemies in superfluous hair, or peel onions up-wind of their trenches to blind them with tears.

Right: cartoon from the German magazine *Simplicissimus* soon after Italy's entry into the war. Poor Italy; on different sides in two World Wars, but always depicted undersized and over-feathered.

Avanti, Savoia!

There were a few good cartoonists at work in Britain, among them W. Heath Robinson, whose drawings still make us laugh; though mildly malicious towards all, they are vicious towards none. The silhouettes at the ends of our chapters come from his *Some Frightful War Pictures* and *The Saintly Hun.*

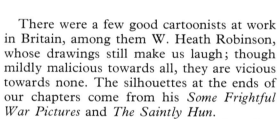

Others were much more enterprising. The German *Simplicissimus* used colour (*Punch* was in black and white only) and between the jokes and cartoons were pictures of girls waving goodbye to submarines or kissing glamorous officers, and nostalgic scenes of the *Heimatland;* all very pretty, but usually without the visual impact of the German posters.

The pages of the French *La Baïonnette* were marvellously varied. There were comic strips, bold vivid cartoons (sometimes very vicious) and lots of decorative and pretty drawings of girls. The jokes about the war are not mealy-mouthed and are often very penetrating. Some of the artists (especially Iribe, Gallo and Wegener) were brilliant, and it is good that they are at last becoming better known.

By 1914, 20,000,000 people a week went to the cinema in Britain—a tempting audience for a government pregnant with messages. The film industry was curiously slow to become involved, but eventually, with official encouragement, it played its part. Film cartoons like those of Lancelot Speed (a fast worker if ever there was one) showed horrid Huns striding jerkily across Europe and being bested by noble Tommies. In one cartoon Bonzo the bulldog defeated a nasty little ogre called German Frightfulness, and an official film was entitled *Once a German, Always a German.* Eventually it was realized that the war was a heaven-sent subject for feature films and the industry cashed in. Charlie Chaplin, everyone's favourite, made a full-length feature *Shoulder Arms.* Though many thought that he had taken a great risk, since the film guyed soldiering, it was an enormous success.

The cult of the heroes and leaders was popular in every country and was used for every purpose from private worship to public propaganda, in every type from the stern father-figure of Hindenburg to the glamorous young air aces, in every medium from bronze to soap (a bust of Kitchener modelled in Margerison's White Windsor Soap figured on an advertising postcard). Effigies of national heroes came in every size from statues twenty metres high to lapel buttons, and in every degree of realism from chip-carvings to waxworks. The courage with which amateurs plunged into portraiture was as amazing as the results—no Royal Academician ever made a better portrait of King George V than the little figure on this page made of sugar-cane leaves (and what professional sculptor would ever have ventured upon such an intractable material?).

THE PROUDEST MOMENT OF HIS LIFE

Top: leaders were idolized in many ways and in every medium. The wasp-waisted general is done in chip-carving reminiscent of African work; he was found in South Wales. *Right:* Jellicoe and Kitchener painted in grisaille on glass. *Opposite:* 'The Proudest Moment of his Life' (signed 'Gladys'), showing King George V pinning the VC on an Australian soldier, one of several groups made by the same lady. We have been told that making figures of this type out of sugar-cane leaves used to be a folk-craft in Queensland, so perhaps that is where Gladys came from.

Left: sculpture by French soldiers at Aveluy, where a chalk cliff has been covered with the carvings of the bored; the work of several hands —the nude surely by a professional.

Opposite. Top: this Sopwith Camel was the thousandth aeroplane turned out by Ruston's works in Lincoln, England. It was blazoned with the Behudet, the Egyptian winged sun, eyed like the ships of the ancient seafarers. Popular decoration, always elaborate, relished the exotic. *Bottom:* the traditional art-forms of the various countries soon embraced the new subject matter.

欧洲大戦乱畫報（其三）獨佛兩軍（ミュール）（ハウセン）大激戰

Flags wagged everywhere. They were bright and beautiful, simple and recognizable, and artists loved to use them. The origins of their heraldry were forgotten, so they were infinitely adaptable to a variety of situations—ready in a moment to advertise chocolates, drape an allegorical matron, cover the corpse of a hero. Friendly flags snapped briskly in the breeze, enemy flags drooped miserably in tatters. Devaluation of the old mystical symbols had of course started long previously: the use of a picture of Queen Victoria to advertise a commercial product would have been unthinkable at the time of her coronation, but by her son's coronation there he was on a postcard drinking Horniman's Tea. The British national flag, like the Royal face, was no longer a sacred totem available solely for patriotic purposes and it had been widely used to advertise things that had absolutely no connection with it. This combination of jingoism and commerce continued cheerfully throughout the war: the little round cardboard boxes of Union Jack Corn Cure, which had been on sale for years, reached their hey-day when popped into parcels to bring relief to marching feet.

Indeed, flags are so splendid that although they are disregarded or decried from time to time, they keep finding new life. The Union Jack, for one, had a great popular revival in the 1960s on shopping bags, mugs, and even neckties and umbrellas. (Some nations have always remained pretty solemn about their flag—witness the disastrous failure of an enterprising but ill-informed Briton who tried to sell Old Glory knickers as souvenirs to American troops in the Second World War.)

Manufacturers liked to give an up-to-date, wartime, ready-to-go air to their advertisements ('Not only is it excellent, but it is patriotic to buy it,' was the implication), and they used tanks, aeroplanes, soldiers, shells—anything—often with rhyme but usually without reason.

Opposite: Allied flag-wagging. The little pin-cushion is worked in wool cross-stitch, with the flag on both sides. The five cubes of the Allied Flags Puzzle have to be arranged so that no two flags repeat in any row; and the superb plate by W. H. Goss has flags at their simple best. *Middle left:* no flags, but belligerent Allies advertising steel toe-caps for boots. *Middle right:* an Italian card with the British officer mysteriously dressed in field grey. All the officers are briskly moustached and at least 7 ft. tall. *Bottom left:* flags again, this time as playing cards. Nap was a popular card game. *Bottom right:* an early card of 1914, designed when it would be all over by Christmas.

Star Protectors
for Your Sole Benefit

IT'S A "NAP HAND."

CHEER, BOYS, CHEER !!   WE'LL ALL MEET
IN BERLIN !

The men who dreamed up the objects and images in this book varied in their attitudes to reality. Whether they were designing for factory production or for themselves, they had to start from some sort of source material. Sometimes they actually saw the objects they portrayed, and then worked from memory; sometimes they only saw them in newspaper pictures or on postcards; sometimes they may never have seen any visual representation, but merely have heard or read about them. There can seldom have been scale drawings to work from; when there were, the result was probably a scale model, a type of craftwork with entirely different intentions—few of the things in this book are scale models, and where they are, translation into a different (often unsuitable) material lends its own kind of unreality.

It is unlikely that all the distortion was due to lack of information; where the subject was simple in shape and well publicized, the mad variety of results must surely have sprung from invention and imagination. Where decoration (often splendidly irrelevant) was added, we may be sure that copying was not the intention. Many of the trench-made objects were very small, perhaps so that they could easily be slipped into a pocket; but perhaps they were deliberately made tiny to minimize the horror of what they represented, reduced to something that could be wrapped up and put out of mind. But some of the wilder models, despite being pocket-sized, became through emotion and distortion con-

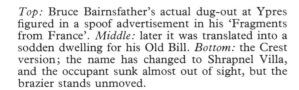

Top: Bruce Bairnsfather's actual dug-out at Ypres figured in a spoof advertisement in his 'Fragments from France'. *Middle:* later it was translated into a sodden dwelling for his Old Bill. *Bottom:* the Crest version; the name has changed to Shrapnel Villa, and the occupant sunk almost out of sight, but the brazier stands unmoved.

22

siderable evocations of power. Whatever prompted such distortion and fantasy in the trench artists, the range of expression is extraordinary. Similarly, on the home front imagination produced fantastic versions of the bare facts—the artist of the Japanese print, excited by the great possibilities of aerial warfare, reverted to a pre-war style of science-fiction illustration, while a manufacturer of one of the actual new weapons, the aeroplane, turned it back 4000 years or so to ancient Egypt, well before the post-war discovery of Tutankhamen's tomb made the style fashionable (p. 19).

It is clear that most people were happier not using the facts. The trench artists had the facts all round them, and distorted them away to what was obviously their hearts' content, in mad mazes of fretwork, appliqué and inlay. But one is bound to ask why more artists away from the front did not use the facts, since surely they were available to them through photography, established as a recording medium for wars since the Crimea? The answer is that the camera lied, that it was made to lie. We now expect the instant publication of horrific photographs, but the photographs and films of 1914–18 were heavily censored, so that the results were as sweet and tame as the censor pleased, showing a very strange war where mud and blood hardly existed, a war as fantastic as the zaniest pop, though much duller. It was not until the Thirties that the suppressed photographs appeared.

Top: Canadian Official Postcard of late 1916 entitled 'Tank going into action'. *Upper middle:* Crest tanks showed the Mark I with two steering-wheels, and a Mark V with no steering wheels, but there was also an improbable version with a single off-set wheel; such a tank was never manufactured —it wouldn't have worked. *Lower middle:* a cast-iron money-box also had one wheel, but it was a very one-sided design, with sponson and guns also on one side only. Could these models be derived from the Canadian postcard, which is plainly a faked action picture based on a wrecked tank? And could the tank in the postcard be the one in the bottom photograph, taken a year later with the graves of its crew nearby?

Top: six panels from a pull-out cartoon based on the Bayeux Tapestry—Wilhelm the non-Conqueror. The border to panel 3 is a reminder of the pre-eminence of the German optical industry; a crafty cryptogram in panel 4 got an Anglo-Saxon mono-syllable into print years before Lady Chatterley. *Bottom:* one of a series of German medals, solidly well-designed, which showed heroes, leaders, Siegfried, Neptune, a Zeppelin passing over Tower Bridge, a caricature of a British press baron sharpening his pen on a huge nutmeg grater (joke now lost), and finally this one, 'America's Contribution to the War', by Ludwig Gies. Uncle Sam, just recognizable by his hat, is a braying ass-ship, stuffed with dollars and carrying munitions past a pretty group of sky-scrapers.

Truth was at a discount throughout the Great War. The lies were told in speeches, pictures, films, toys, newspapers, in every medium from the grandest to the most trivial. The suppression of the photographs of mass-slaughter came easily enough to a generation brought up in nineteenth-century prudery which drew a veil not only over sex but also over the fact of death (though it was unrestrained about its trappings—mourning and monuments were lavish). Although lives were poured away like water, everything was done to make the deaths invisible. Today we can see that the 600,000 casualties of Verdun were a criminal and un-forgivable waste even by the dubious standards of war. In 1916, though, it was a 'great victory' for France—the few dissident voices were suppressed.

For decades before 1914, literary fantasies published all over Europe had envisaged the next war. Though the battles described in them were outmoded and utterly unlike the eventual reality, they propagated precisely those myths of atrocities and barbarity that were churned out in every medium once the war started. Anti-German fever in Britain was so ruthlessly worked up that the windows of shops with German names were smashed, harmless waiters and governesses of German nationality were persecuted, Prince Louis of Battenburg lost his job and King George V changed his German surname to Windsor. People reacted with frightening predictability to every stimulus, laughing at the comic German pig, turning white with hate at the brutalities of the bloody Hun.

24

HELM: GIVETH ORDERS FOR FRIGHTFULNESS
THUNDER WEATHER YES!

HE TRIETH THE AIR

HERE HE HANDETH IRON CROSSES
MILITARY WILHELM
CLERK

From 1914 to 1918 the Allies were so bludgeoned with lies, later disproved, that factual accounts of the major horrors of Hitler's Germany were later shrugged off as just so much propaganda—the old story of Wolf! Wolf! (It really should have been the British and not the German propaganda agency that was called the Wolff Bureau.)

Hateful or ridiculous images of the enemy were as constant a feature of propaganda as heroic images—we shall look at some of them later. The variety is immense, but they have one factor in common: they all come from the hands of professionals. The amateurs stuck to the heroes. There is no technical reason for this—surely the fangs and blood and claws, the stock-in-trade for beastly enemy images, could present no problem to men who dealt so un-

hesitatingly with the fierce moustaches and whiskers of their leaders. Amateur artists are often much bolder than professionals in attempting subjects filled with raw emotion and since hatred is an emotion particularly in evidence in wartime one might reasonably expect to find thousands of amateur works of art expressing it. We have found none.

The objects made in the trenches show more love for whittling than hatred of the enemy; the things filled with hate were made far from the front line. The trench artists present a war as remote from reality as the official communiqués and photographs, a world purged of mud and blood and hatred. If the popular arts of the First World War tell us anything encouraging about people, this is it.

US & THEM

It is important in war never to see your enemy as a human being; why, you might think he was just like you, and not want to kill him at all. On Christmas Day 1914 firing stopped, and men, still seeing the enemy as other men, went out into no-man's-land and exchanged drinks and chocolate, and played football. The High Commands were very angry and such weakness was not allowed again.

The easiest way not to see the enemy as a man was to see him as something else—a comic sausage, a cowardly cur, a brute beast of any sort. Then, after being trained to charge with a bayonet at a stuffed sack, screaming on the run, everyone had an excellent chance of becoming sub-human himself, and dog could eat dog. But of course it would never do to admit to being a brute yourself, so as well as making vile stereotypes of the enemy, each side made noble ones of its own combatants.

All allies were goodies: handsome, virile, clean and upstanding. All enemies were baddies: ugly, depraved, filthy and fanged. Switch the uniforms of the heroic stereotypes of the two sides, and one would do for the other, though the German heroes tend to be bonier than the others, just as the Italians are sexier.

When the artists got tired of drawing the stereotypes, they could always fall back on the national allegorical figures. Germania and Britannia were remarkably alike, mature ladies with stern faces, wearing bits of classical armour over insecure draperies—images centuries old. France had Marianne, a hoyden in a scarlet cap of liberty, usually waving an antique sword rather than a gun. All these could easily be turned by the other side into figures of fun, cowardice or horror. And so could the animals. Britain saw its lion standing proudly lashing its tail; Germany saw him starved and mangy, barely able to lift a paw.

26

Das europäische Gleichgewicht — nach einjährigem Kampf.

"DEUTSCHLAND · ÜBER · ALLES"!
"Germany over all"—(We don't think!)

The tamer sort of propaganda postcard from the early part of the war, before feelings ran really high. *Top:* a German card showing two normal, healthy soldiers of the Central Powers staring in amazement at a sorry jumble of deformed and paralysed Allies in archaic uniforms. For once, Italy is allowed to show fight. *Bottom:* an even tamer and smugger British card by Donald McGill, with none of his usual gusto. Everybody is spick and span, including the Kaiser, whose gloves are as white as the Russian's tunic.

27

Für's Vaterland!
OTTO SAGER
BLN-STEGLITZ
Freikorps
Loeschebrand
der Garde-Kav.-Schützen-Division
Annahmestelle für Freiwillige
Berlin, Kantstr. 162, nahe Bahnhof Zoologischer-Garten.

As people see themselves and as others see them. *Left:* a soberly heroic Teutonic image (there were plenty of more musclebound Siegfrieds and busty Germanias to match John Bull and Britannia). *Right:* a German soldier through Italian eyes.

Kaiser Franz Josef I.

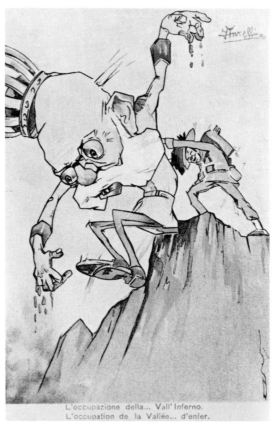

L'occupazione della... Vall' Inferno.
L'occupation de la Vallée... d'enfer.

1914

L'ENVOYÉ DE DIEU

Pierre Châtillon
1915

Top: poor old Franz Josef through (pre-war) Austrian and through (wartime) Italian eyes. *Bottom:* the Kaiser through Austrian and through French eyes.

Top: a *Bersagliere* photographed in full plumage, and a German version from *Simplicissimus*. *Bottom:* the British Lion, also from *Simplicissimus*.

The hostile stereotypes, both human and animal, used by each side to vilify the other had one thing in common—they all recognized that the enemy had it in him to do a certain amount of damage. With one exception— Italy. For some reason poor Italy was usually portrayed as useless and undersized—an outsize *Bersagliere* hat swamped in enormous feathers emphasizing the point. The Italians certainly hit back, and produced the most bile-jerking graphics of the whole war (see the postcards on pages 52 and 53).

The Decline of the Heroic Image.
Top left and right: Le Bluet, by Mlle. G. Achille Fould, exhibited at the Paris Salon, and another Bluet, by Marco de Gastyne, from *La Baïonnette*, 4 May 1916: 'Think that two months ago, mother used to bring me cocoa in bed!' *Bottom left and right:* the fearless, dashing Briton, too splendid even to be labelled Tommy Atkins, gave way to Bruce Bairnsfather's Old Bill.

Left: an Australian recruiting poster by Norman Lindsay, with a rougher, tougher and altogether more practical image than was usual in such posters, but still undeniably heroic. *Right:* by 1916 the Australians were prepared to see themselves as even rougher, and unheroic by anybody's standards.

As the war went on, the heroic images of Allied graphics changed dramatically. The comic artists, much in demand to cheer everyone up, created stereotypes of a new sort, asinine officers, raw recruits gormless among the old soldiers, the old sweats themselves, tough, indomitable, making the best of it, but dirty and cynical.

The best British old soldier was Bruce Bairnsfather's Old Bill, a gloomy man with a walrus moustache. The most famous drawing shows him with another soldier in a shell hole in no-man's-land with more shells bursting all around; the caption is 'Well, if you knows of a better 'ole, go to it!' Captain Bairnsfather's drawings were published weekly in the *Bystander* and as postcards, prints and calendars—their appeal seems to have been universal—and they were collected in a series called *Fragments from France*. In number 2 of the series a photograph 'straight off the mud' shows Bairnsfather with fur coat,

Balaclava helmet, gum-boots and a pipe, in front of a shell hole; he drew what he saw about him, and himself wore the full 'old soldier' outfit, slightly modified for an officer. His fed-up, unkempt soldiers collectively turned into a new heroic image, which contained a truth and a humanity missing in the vapid stereotypes of 1914. The editor of the *Bystander*, who had been responsible for propagating this surprising new image (surprising because an increase in truthfulness is rare in wartime) wrote, 'These *verdammte Englander* are never what they seem, but are always something unpleasantly different. We are the Great Enigma of the war, and in our mystery lies our greatest strength'—a smug and pompous statement utterly out of tune with Old Bill's cynical realism.

Old Bill had his Allied counterparts. The French, in *La Baïonnette*, produced their own scruffy realists, like the quaking lad opposite and the cynics on page 113.

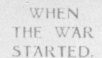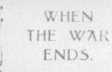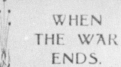

WHEN THE WAR STARTED.   WHEN THE WAR ENDS.   WHEN THE WAR STARTED.   WHEN THE WAR ENDS.

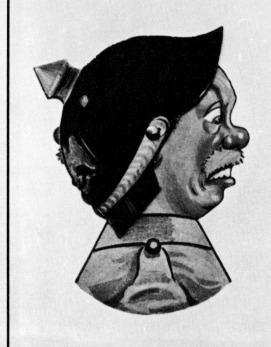

TAKEN THREE DAYS LEAVE.   GOT SIX DAYS "C.B."   TAKEN THREE DAYS LEAVE.   GOT SIX DAYS "C.B."

Two kindly British postcards poking the same sort of simple fun at two simple men. The helmets swivel on pins to change the men's expressions from glad to sad.

The Central Powers do not seem to have allowed their popular images to decline in the same way. Diligent searches have produced no parallels to the examples on the previous page. One German artist, a Professor Schmidt, depicted his own side as Neanderthal men with low brows and prognathous jaws. He churned out paintings for reproduction in German magazines, mostly of battle scenes in which his primordial soldiery are shown tearing into fleeing French infantry. But he was not pop, and not at all funny.

The United States was not involved in the fighting for long enough to experience a similar decline from the early heady heroics. Their turn came in the Second World War, in which Bill Mauldin's unshaven, gum-chewing GIs were the only true descendants of Bairnsfather's muddy grumblers.

In the first years of the war there was a surprising (and comforting) vein of non-beastly portrayals of the enemy—they were not always shown as monsters dripping with blood. There are, of course, very few dead straight portraits, though the French produced a series of postcards in 1914 of typical Allied and Central Powers soldiers in which both sides are similarly treated—a touch of caricature here and there, but not only of the opposition. The bearded Bavarian in the series is a very amiable uncle with a curly pipe.

Those portrayals of the enemy that were not beastly were mostly comic, but many of the artists presented both sides with similar touches of ridicule. Heath Robinson's Germans were certainly comic, but so were his Tommies. Bairnsfather's Germans were usually considerably under- or over-weight, and tended to have their hair cut extremely short, but then Old Bill was hardly the acme of male beauty.

The Tommies in *Simplicissimus* are tall and thin and very bony (surprisingly like the ones in *La Baïonnette*) but they are not monsters. They are usually dejected as a result of being misled and out-manoeuvred (not an unrealistic portrait, on the whole), and the artists seem to have been sorry for their predicament.

This mood of comparative reasonableness did not last long; the climate of opinion favoured the hate-makers, and they prevailed.

YOU'RE IN THE ARMY NOW

You're in the army now, boy,
You're not behind the plow;
You'll never get rich
You son of a bitch
You're in the army now.

(Popular song, USA)

The combatant nations entered the war with varying proportions of their male populations trained to fight. Germany and France had a lot; Britain and the United States very few; the British Dominions even fewer. The regulars and the part-timers knew what soldiering was about, but most of those who eventually participated had never been closer to army life than when, as small boys, they had skipped through the streets behind military bands—an unruly and unsoldierly tailpiece to the stirring precision of brass and drum.

At first the call went out for volunteers; by the end, most countries had introduced conscription. By whatever means they came to enlist, millions entered a new world of experience. At first there was the unfamiliar environment of barracks, huts and tents, and eventually a move far from home, probably to foreign parts, itself a new experience for most. There was a strange new routine from reveille to lights-out, and discipline of a type unknown in even the strictest factory, farm or office. Fierce personages, who knew it all, barked and chivvied and rebuked—corporals; drill sergeants; musketry instructors. Officers were remote and beyond communication.

There were new tasks to be undertaken. A man who had always left peeling the spuds to the little woman suddenly found himself peeling a ton; the unwashed were made to wash; the timid and retiring joined the bellicose extroverts in uttering strange cries and sticking bayonets into effigies of the foe. The unmechanical were by turns threatened, cajoled and railed at until they had mastered the mechanism of the service rifle. 'Treat your rifle like a wife' was sound advice but bleak compensation for disrupted domesticity.

They complained endlessly, but the grousing was a form of verbal therapy rather than serious protest. Their grumbles about foot-slogging, ill-fitting uniforms, living in tents, sergeants and army food were translated into cartoons, jokes, songs and postcards.

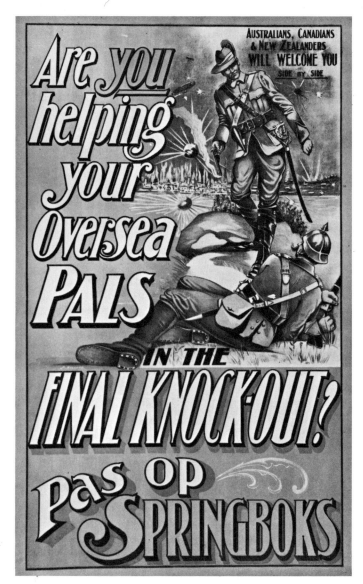

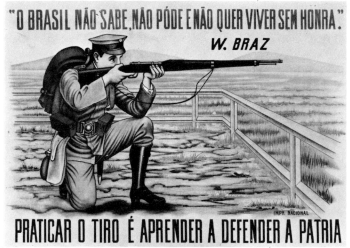

Above: a South African recruiting poster in the best vernacular tradition of elaboration, with superb lettering. The Springbok was promised a place SIDE BY SIDE with Australians, Canadians and New Zealanders; no truck with Limeys or Wops, Frogs or Wogs. *Top right:* Brazilians are exhorted to rifle practice in defence of their homeland. *Below:* an Australian echo of the pointing finger in Alfred Leete's world famous Kitchener image. *Next page:* one of H. M. Bateman's funniest cartoons, here reproduced from *La Baïonnette,* 17 January 1918, shows the response of cowboy Big Bill to President Wilson's call to arms; even the wolves who chase him are pressed into service, and he finally takes his medical coming down the home straight.

(Dessin de Bateman.)

COMMENT BI

...NDIT A L'APPEL.

News and Views
from
Salisbury Plain.

I'VE ARRIVED AT LITTLEHAMPTON

1340

O welche Lust Soldat zu sein.

Drummer Bent was awarded the V. C. for conspicuous bravery near Le Gheer on November 1st and 2nd, when after all his Officers had been struck down he took command and succeeded in holding the position.
Previously he had distinguished himself by bringing up ammunition.— And again on Nov. 3rd by rescueing Pte McNulty under heavy shell and rifle fire.

Vaudville theatre – Interior

Once in, the recruit found everything very different from the posters, and the boredom and exhaustion of drill in heavy boots were expressed for him in countless comic postcards to send home. They show him sweating under gigantic packs, or, heavy with irony, waiting for his sergeant to bring the morning tea.

Opposite. Left: the pull-out zig-zags of little views continued as in peace-time; Salisbury Plain had always been used for manoeuvres, and views of the camps were ready to hand. Other places with new camps, like Littlehampton, still showed the views of local beauty spots that had been used in pre-war cards. *Top right:* it was just the same on the other side. *Centre right:* to make all the square-bashing seem worth while, there were dreams of glory, a chance at the great deeds that were celebrated in every popular medium. This is one of a set of six 'scraps', which were bought in sheets and separated for the album. Each shows a different winner of the Victoria Cross.

Bottom right: one of a set of six advertising post-cards, each showing Victoria Cross winners. In each, a crate of Walker, Harrison & Garthwaites biscuits just happens to be at the point of action—even, in one case, in a German trench.

This page. Top: a theatre for British troops in Italy. Man's almost universal desire to alleviate and decorate his surroundings produced friezes of cut-out grapes, trellis-work, and even palms to make all as cosy as possible. *Bottom:* 'Mr Malcolm Scott is selling his photographs for the benefit of the brave men at-the-Front. The money received is devoted to sending 1/- parcels (really 3/6 worth) . . . And one of these photographs is enclosed in each parcel to liven up a Dug-out. Will you help to make the men happy?'

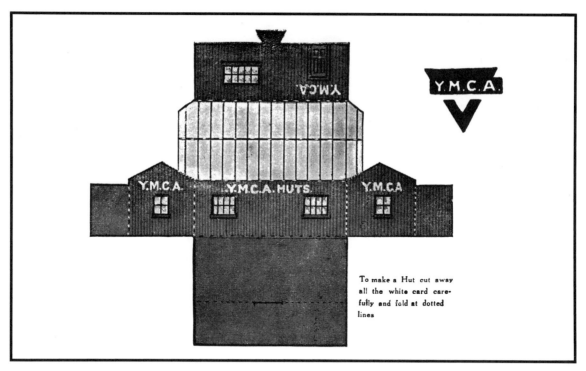

To make a Hut cut away all the white card carefully and fold at dotted lines

The Young Men's Christian Association built recreation rooms for the troops, often the only amenity for miles. Funds were raised on Hut Days by selling flags, and cards like this one to cut out and fold up into a little grey hut for the mantelpiece.

There were, of course, compensations. Uniforms, though soberer than in former wars, were thought glamorous, and invested even an undersized weed with a new status in the community. For the more ambitious, there were dreams of glory, fed by newspaper accounts of heroic deeds. For the less romantic there was at least a sense of camaraderie and duty strong enough to carry them, in the years ahead, through unimagined nightmares.

There were more basic compensations too. Apart from the wine, women and chips provided by private enterprise, there were philanthropic organizations, whose huts and clubs brought relaxation, tea and buns to millions. And because man cannot live on buns alone, cultural fare was offered by touring concert parties in makeshift theatres. When they were beyond the reach of such organized entertainment in remote overseas stations, on board ship, or in prison camps, the troops entertained themselves, and with home-made wigs and false breasts did their best to make up for the lack of female talent.

PROPAGANDA & MORALE

The cover of the French comic paper *La Baïonnette*, volume iv, has a new interpretation of the pen beating the sword, with Marianne (as usual more active than Britannia) charging with a giant pencil instead of a bayonet. Both sides did their best to make this concept true.

In 1622 the Roman Catholic Church founded the College of Propaganda to oversee foreign missions; by 1842 the word 'propaganda' covered any scheme to propagate any practice. Its use in wartime completed its descent to a dirty word—deceit is now implicit in it. From 1914 on, both sides claimed the same victories, multiplied the numbers of enemy captured or killed, divided their own, and invented as many out-and-out lies as seemed expedient. Most people believed them implicitly. In Britain, for instance, photographs were published of a factory in Germany where corpses were boiled down for fat, and everyone knew someone who had seen with his own eyes a German cutting off a Belgian baby's hands, or a Canadian officer crucified to a barn door with bayonets.

"WAKE UP!"
A DREAM OF TO-MORROW.

It shows the cold-blooded murder of a little boy who had aimed his small toy gun at some of the invading enemy.

This is a scene from the great "Daily Express" Patriotic Film, "Wake Up!" by Laurence Cowen.

Freundschaftsanbahnung eines grossen "Barbaren" mit einem belgischen Miniatursoldaten.

This page. Top left: a pre-war anticipation of atrocity propaganda. *Top right:* to counter the 'Hun' image, the Germans showed this nice 'Barbarian' making firm friends with a Belgian child. *Bottom:* hatred always to hand; this metal top to a walking stick shows a French soldier strangling a German.

Opposite. Top left: the German Crown Prince, 'Little Willie', came in for more sneers than hate. *Middle left:* contrasting hate pieces; German, 'Our work is God's work. Right is our judge.' French, 'Suffer little children to come unto me!!!' (those hand-less Belgian children again). *Right:* an American poster, 1918; one of the few uses of sex in Great War propaganda graphics—seeing that every other below-the-belt trick was exploited, how odd that they didn't use it more. *Bottom:* a French pre-war postcard of one of the famous gargoyles on Notre Dame, and the same photograph given the Kaiser's head. Next, a nasty French card of a soldier strangling what one can only hope is a stuffed eagle. Last, a postcard published in Egypt, showing the Kaiser fenced in by the fickle fingers of fate.

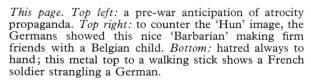

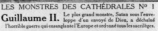

MARTYRE DE MISS EDITH CAVELL
12 Octobre 1915.

REMEMBER!

Top: a French postcard; an imaginary scene of the 'Martyrdom of Miss Edith Cavell'. The legend on the back translates 'Condemned to death by a military tribunal in Belgium, for having helped English and Belgian soldiers to escape, Miss Edith Cavell of Norwich, a voluntary nurse, is led to the place of execution at dawn on 12 October. She faints. The German officer gives his soldiers the order to fire; they refuse to fire on the panting body of a woman. The gold-braided monster draws his revolver and leans over the victim and coolly blows her brains out.' *Bottom left:* Crest figure of Edith Cavell. *Bottom right:* another French postcard shows 'Rammler, a German soldier, shot for refusing to fire on Miss Edith Cavell'. Another legend?

EDITH CAVELL
BRUSSELS
DAWN
OCTOBER 12TH
1915

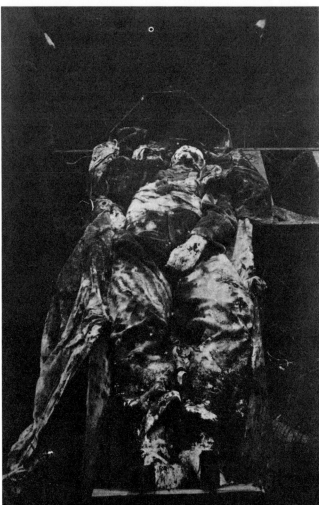

Sometimes there were awkward mistakes: the same photograph of the same burnt-out Zeppelin shed was claimed by the Germans to be Russian and by the British to be German. But truth was usually manipulated to give the clear message—We are good and They are bad. It appeared in every medium: film, theatre, books of fiction or 'fact', newspapers. Sometimes it was not necessary to invent anything at all. For instance, the Kaiser played straight into the propagandists' hands by telling his troops embarking for Peking in 1900, 'When you meet the foe you will defeat him. No quarter will be given, no prisoners will be taken . . . Gain a reputation like the Huns of Attila.' Plenty of people remembered *that* indiscretion.

From force of habit even the most pertinent truth was embellished. The story of Nurse Edith Cavell illustrates this. She ran a clinic in Brussels, and continued to do so after the Germans occupied the city. She was asked to hide some British soldiers, and by the summer of 1915 had become the Brussels link in an underground escape line. She was efficient but apparently careless, so that the Germans became suspicious. They planted an agent posing as a French doctor, and in due course arrested and shot her. They could claim that the rules of war justified this, but it turned out to have been unwise, as it confirmed to the whole world the Hun image. Her last words to the chaplain were, 'I know now that patriotism is not enough. I must have no hatred and no bitterness toward anyone.'

The Allied propaganda machine went straight into action whipping up patriotic indignation in a precisely contrary spirit. There were stories of a German soldier who was executed for refusing to shoot her, and of the whole firing squad refusing so that the officer had to shoot her in the head. A series of fantasy paintings about her by an Italian artist, T. Corbella, was exhibited at the Leicester Galleries in London (see page 52).

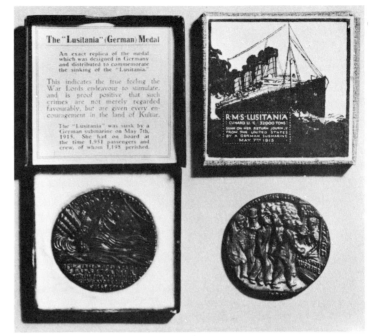

Top: a Munich silversmith struck a medal, designed by K. Goetz, to commemorate the sinking of the *Lusitania* with over 1000 non-combatants (and some munitions). It showed Death sitting in the Cunard office selling tickets, a passenger with a newspaper carrying the words U-BOAT DANGER, and a bearded German wagging a warning finger. On the reverse, the decks of the sinking ship are heaped with guns and aircraft. Inscriptions—BUSINESS AS USUAL and NO CONTRABAND. In retaliation, the British set up a '*Lusitania* Souvenir Medal Committee' which distributed replicas packaged in anti-German sentiments. One such replica is illustrated above.

Bottom: joke Iron Crosses made in Britain bearing the names of Belgian towns bombarded by the Germans, and the word *Kultur* to scorn the Kaiser's claim to be spreading German culture. The large one has a portrait of him flanked by Frankfurter sausages; the one at the top, pressed in bronze, is inscribed 'The Kaiser's Very Cross'. (Mounted and framed by Bill Howell.)

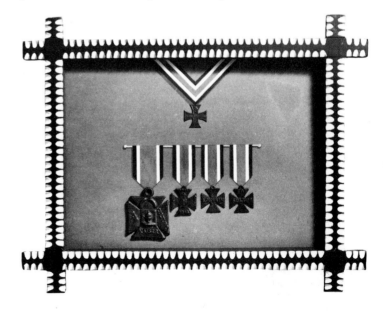

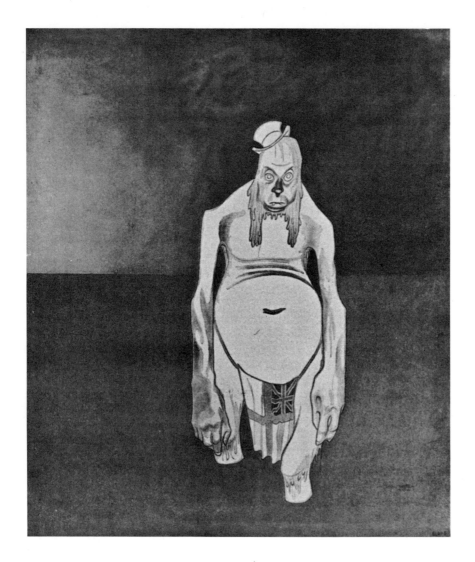

Above: a German cartoon of a sorrowful John Bull in a Union Jock-strap slinking back from the Battle of Jutland. Both sides claimed a resounding victory—the British lost more ships, but the German fleet never effectively put to sea again.
Opposite. Left: A German poster by Otto Lehman, 'Support our Field Greys. Bend England's Might. Subscribe to the War Loan.' *Right:* for a contrast in graphics, an English advertising calendar which might have been designed fifty years earlier; many of the details are Edwardian Baroque, but the elaboration is purely nineteenth-century. About thirty of Messrs Barbour's fabrics, civil and military, are listed, entwined with fourteen Allied flags, six British Empire ones, three trade marks, the King, the Viceroy, Haig, Jellicoe, Beatty, HMS *Victory*, England Expects, guns, aircraft, the calendar for 1917, 2 tridents for the supremacy of the seas and Best Wishes. Everything but the artist's name.

Next page: a very nasty double spread from *La Baïonnette*, 8 June 1916, 'After war—misery . . . Off to the human rubbish heap!' A prophetic French view of post-war Germany; the Nazi movement grew from precisely this rubbish heap.

APRES LA GU...
Gare à la ...

... LA MISÈRE...
humaine !...

(Dessin de Zislin)

First great german victory. — Première grande victoire allemande.

THE "PALS".

THESE RUSSIAN BALLETS ARE FATIGUEING

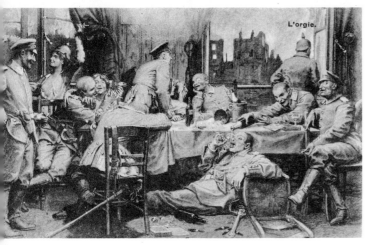

L'orgie.

Rome 25 Septembre 1914.

La lettre du Pape

Benoît XV
à
Guillaume.

En détruisant les
temples de Dieu,
vous provoquez
la colère divine,
devant laquelle
les armées les
plus puissantes
perdent tout pou-
voir

Pinx S. Solomko.
Reproduction interdite.
1752   M. L.

This page. Top left: one of a set of French cards showing the rape of Belgium by the German army. Whether or not the Germans missed any tricks, the artists certainly did not; rape, shooting of prisoners, advancing behind a screen of civilians (including nude ones), it's all in the series. *Top right:* for those with less lurid tastes, French manufacturers also played on religious sentiments; 'Letter from Pope Benedict XV to William —By destroying the houses of God you have aroused that divine wrath before which the mightiest armies are powerless.' *Bottom:* from an Italian postcard entitled 'The Turnip the Prussians Wish to Plant in Paris'; it looks as if it's going to hurt.

Opposite: Hate. *Top:* a silver-plated *pickelhaube* inkwell run through with a sword, and a Crest Tommy driving a steamroller over the Kaiser. *Middle. Left:* one postcard of a series of six based on paintings by T. Corbella of Rome, making a fanciful myth out of the Cavell execution. This one entitled 'A Birthday Present for the Kaiser', shows Death offering the nurse's head on a salver. *Right:* 'The First Great German Victory' (French). *Bottom:* more cracks at the Kaiser. *Bottom right:* One of a Tuck series based on *Aesop's Fables*, here reprinted for the Portuguese market.

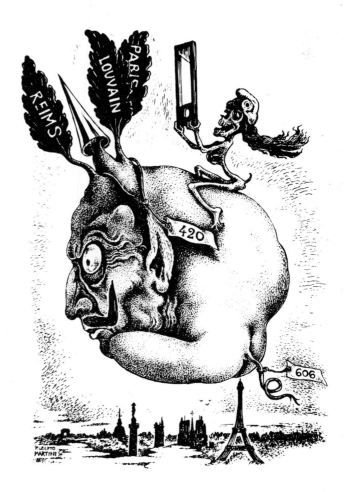

Much propaganda was concerned with ordering and exhorting the civilian population—black your windows out, save food, walls have ears, save till it hurts, buy war bonds, eat your crusts. As the war dragged on, and the glory was found to have gone away, straight morale-boosting became the sacred duty. The terrible casualty lists were not offset by any visible progress—thousands of men on both sides died to move the front line a hundred yards. So to encourage the soldiers as well as the armchair strategists who tired of scarcely moving the little coloured flags on their maps, every last drop was squeezed from heroes, martyrs and atrocities. On the one side there was the *Lusitania*, on the other the blockading of German ports and the starving of civilians.

The flood of professional and amateur propaganda was ceaseless. As early as September 1914 William le Queux wrote '*German Atrocities. A Record of Shameless Deeds*', which included both 'eye-witness' accounts of all those atrocities which are only committed by the other side and poems like 'The Day' by Henry Chappell, a porter known as the Railway Poet of Bath. Here are four verses of diatribe against the Kaiser:

You spied for the Day, you lied for the Day,
And woke the Day's red spleen.
Monster, who asked God's aid Divine,
Then strewed His seas with the ghastly mine;
Not all the waters of the Rhine
Can wash thy foul hands clean.

You dreamed for the Day, you schemed for the
   Day;
Watch how the Day will go.
Slayer of age and youth and prime
(Defenceless slain for never a crime),
Thou art steeped in blood as a hog in slime,
False friend and cowardly foe.

You have sown for the Day, you have grown
   for the Day;
Yours is the harvest red.
Can you hear the groans and the awful cries?
Can you see the heap of slain that lies,
And sightless turned to the flame-split skies
The glassy eyes of the dead?

But after the Day there's a price to pay
For the sleepers under the sod,
And He you have mocked for many a day—
Listen and hear what He has to say:
'Vengeance is mine; I will repay.'
What can you say to God?

MAGIC & MYTH

Even the most unsuperstitious person has at some time touched wood or avoided walking under a ladder. When danger or death are near, or success is earnestly desired, such instincts become very powerful, so that in war people turn to magic symbols and respect taboos (never light three cigarettes from one match—at night a sniper may see the first, aim at the second and fire at the third).

Power was thought to reside in numbers— the Turks believed the strength of a battle ship could be gauged by the number of funnels, and thought nothing of the *Queen Elizabeth* (the most powerful ship that fought against them) because she only had two.

Charms to bring luck were made to be worn on the person; they were depicted on postcards, and used to adorn tanks and aeroplanes. Magic can also be negative, like the white feathers given by patriotic British ladies to men in civilian clothes as symbols of cowardice —white tail feathers in a game bird denote inferior breeding.

Symbols, colours and heraldry were useful to bolster morale and frighten the enemy. Echoes of medieval blazonry frequently burst through the protective drabness—the Germans gave up camouflaging aeroplanes and decorated them with a fine old-fashioned gaudiness. Different colours, of course, had special symbolic value for different nations and were used in different ways; the black and white of the Iron Cross is found in military badges, on greetings postcards, and can still be seen in the lettering of German village war memorials. The British Tank Corps adopted brown, red and green, symbolizing 'through mud and blood to green fields beyond'.

A particular magic was attached in Britain to the Victoria Cross, the highest award for bravery, made of plain bronze and sparingly given. As a symbol it was not so freely used as the German Iron Cross, which went on to everything from Zeppelins to tea-cups. It was not lightly spoken of and seldom joked about; its award was the nearest thing to canonization Britain had seen since the Reformation. It held this status through the Second World War, a very strong magic indeed.

Heroes are singled out by giving them medals—they are 'decorated' just like other special items from altars to Christmas trees. Every nation cultivated its heroes and this mythology sometimes even crossed the front line—von Richthofen, the most famous German airman, was ungrudgingly admired by the Allies.

Heroes and leaders became totems, and were popular on postcards, in china busts and toby jugs. You could even buy a Lord Kitchener door knocker.

Left: charms and mascots. (1) Woollen doll, London. (2) Chinese soapstone monkey carried by British and Japanese troops. (3) Bone fish given to English soldier by Italian friend. (4) Amber heart carried against drowning. (5) Black cat brooch, London. (6) Four-leafed clover and ladybird in locket. (7) Charm for airman. (8) Heart made from spoon-end. (9) Metal cross made from German steel fragments by Belgian soldier. (10) 'Thumbs Up and Touch Wood' combines two very ancient charms. (11) Woollen doll in horseshoe. (12) Metal horseshoe. (13) Nanette, Rintintin and the baby—Parisian charms against bombs. (14) Flint arrowhead sold in USA as lucky charm for a soldier. *Above:* one of the many representations of the Angel of Mons myth. In this painting by W. H. Margetson, angels display their well-known love of fair play by ordering the advancing hordes to give Tommy time to re-load—like a referee holding up the game while someone does up his bootlace.

Opposite. Top left: evidence of more divine intervention; 'This bible saved the life of Private W. Hackett on 20 August 1915, at Armentières'. Beside it, an ambiguous charm; a cross made from a rifle bullet. *Bottom left:* the delicate border-line between heroism and crass stupidity gives an edge to much of the magic. *Right:* Emblems and charms painted on aeroplanes; the shark's teeth on the 1918 Sopwith Dolphin were revived in the Second World War on RAF Tomahawks in the Western Desert and by the Flying Tigers in China.

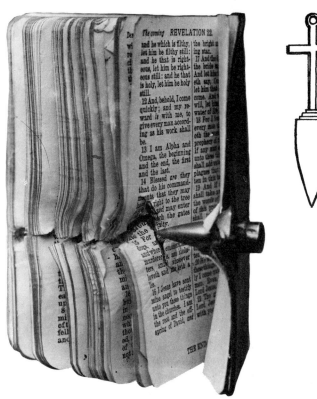

FOOTBALL

KICKED OFF BY

CAPTAIN WILFRED. P. NEVILL

(WHO FELL IN THE ADVANCE)

OF

"B" COMPANY 8ᵗʰ SERVICE BATTALION

EAST SURREY REGIMENT—

AND DRIBBLED INTO THE GERMAN

TRENCHES AT THE ASSAULT

AND CAPTURE OF MONTAUBAN

JULY 1ˢᵗ 1916. ———

(COPYRIGHT.)

In many cultures, sticking pins into effigies is a form of witchcraft aimed at weakening or killing the individual depicted. Not so in Germany, where leaders and heroes were carved in wood, often on a gigantic scale, and nails were bought and driven in to raise money for war charities. *Top left:* this giant Hindenburg was set up in Berlin to raise funds for the National Foundation for the Bereaved of the War. *Top right:* the photograph was reproduced as a postcard, on the back of one of which the sender drew a sketch to show 'My nail'. *Bottom right:* the Captain of the Emden was made in the form of a medieval knight, and filled in with an orderly pattern of nails; it looks as if the genital area was officially filled in first. The custom relates to an ancient one in Nuremberg, where an apprentice leaving the city would drive a nail into a tree in St Stefansplatz—a sort of *Auf Wiedersehen* gesture.

**THE
DIVINE
PERISCOPE**

He died of His Wounds for ME!

Periscopes were used to reflect the view down to a lower, safer, level. This one transmits a message from very high up indeed. In the left background an early fore-runner of

THE BOY HERO OF THE BATTLE OF JUTLAND

Boy, First Class, JOHN TRAVERS CORNWELL V.C. Died June 2nd 1916.
Mortally wounded early in the action, he remained standing alone
at a most exposed post quietly awaiting orders, until the end
of the battle, with the guns crew dead and wounded all round
him. Age, 16½ Years.

Opposite: an idol set up in Paris; a ziggurat of
captured German helmets. *Right:* another cult
figure—Boy Cornwell—featured on a postcard.

The strongest magic of all is religion, so
both sides proclaimed that God was on their
side: every German soldier's belt buckle re-
minded him—*Gott mit uns*. An Allied myth
claimed that angels intervened on their side
at Mons, a curious diversion of truth from the
fact that a miracle had indeed happened—a
miracle of arms by the small British Expedi-
tionary Force whose holding action at Mons
amazed the German High Command. As in
the Second World War, there were myths
about the enemy dressed up as nuns or priests.
There were also more comical myths like the
rumour that the Russians had landed at
Scarborough on their way to help out in
France. Everyone *knew* instinctively they were
Russians, because they all had snow on their
boots.

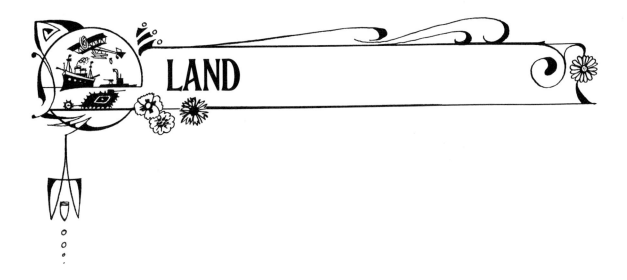

LAND

As Europe blundered into war in the late summer of 1914 everyone knew just what sort of war it was going to be; the Franco-Prussian war of 1870 provided the basic image. Almost all the Jeremiahs and sabre-rattlers who had written about the great European conflict to come had described battles dominated by musketry and cavalry, with squares formed, swords waved, and gunners firing at targets they could actually see (H. G. Wells was one of the few who thought that future wars would be determined by new machines). To right and left of the battle there would be open country, flanks to be turned, space to manoeuvre.

The time scale, too, would have its limits, and battles would be mostly fought between dawn and sunset. A few prophets, remembering Gettysburg, let the decisive confrontation roll on for four days. A continuous four-month-long battle like the Somme or Verdun was never contemplated. The image of 1700 miles of muddy ditches without a man visible above ground level for months on end would have amazed everyone, not least the professional soldiers.

'Over by Christmas' was the firm expecta-tion on both sides. Kitchener, almost alone, foresaw the dark perspective ahead when he said that manpower deployment should be planned on the basis of a three-year war. Many thought he had at last gone off his rocker.

For generals and for postcard artists alike the pattern of war was clear, and the generals started out to fight it in a way that made the artists right. The Battle of the Frontiers in 1914 was fought much as the Japanese artist saw it (on page 19), even if the scale of his air war was somewhat premature.

The weapon which swept infantry and cavalry from the surface of the earth was the machine gun, but it never became a popular image. Though toy makers and the French souvenir industry reproduced it in many forms after the war, it never gained favour with the amateur brass-smiths in the trenches. Perhaps the troops, unlike those safe at home, were restrained by distaste of its ruthless efficiency as a killer. It was left to the official British memorial to the Machine Gun Corps at Hyde Park Corner to commemorate it with the spine-chilling quotation 'Saul slew them in his thousands, but David in his tens of thousands.'

Opposite. Top: the new face of war. A hand-made brass and copper tank; basic features well observed, but proportions haywire—even without the projecting guns it is wider than it is long. The result is a juggernaut image of great power. *Bottom:* a floral cannon greetings card depicts a pretty and kindly war—no mud and blood here.

D*

That Sword.

How he thought he was going to use it——

——and how he did use it.

Opposite: Bruce Bairnsfather neatly summed up the difference between the heroic visions of war and the realities of life in the trenches.

Above: early in the war, amateur battlescapes perpetuated a Franco-Prussian mode of warfare—but then so at first did the generals. *Below:* the grim images of trench warfare took a long time to penetrate into the popular consciousness—hardly surprising when postcards like this German one showed dugouts with rustic fences and roses round the door.

Artillery, on the other hand, was a very popular subject. Models of field guns, howitzers, siege guns, railway guns, proved apt for mantelshelves and effective on the nursery floor. They could be made to work by springs, or, God help us, by actual gunpowder (nursery casualty lists never got published). Many were made of brass, often using the bases of shell cases as wheels; some had barrels made of cartridges. Others had wheels cast or turned, indicating access to workshop machinery. The origin of most of those we have found is impossible to determine—even nationality is unclear; German shell cases could have been used by an Allied soldier. Field and base workshops or factories at home could have provided the lathes; some were no doubt made after the Armistice.

In France the fabulous soixante-quinze, the 75mm field gun of great mobility and a fantastic rate of fire, was made into a sort of patron saint (cannonization!). Photogravure and silk-embroidered postcards proclaimed *Gloire au 75*. Toy ones were made in tin-plate, lead and wood; replicas appeared as flag-day emblems hanging on tricolour ribbons, and in Britain the Crest manufacturers made several versions.

From early in the war, the public was fascinated by armoured cars, even though their participation was marginal. There were several unlikely-looking models in Crest which turn out to be fairly accurate portraits of the strange vehicles, tatted together, surprisingly, by the Royal Naval Air Service in Belgium in the early months of the war.

Here at last were real versions of the fantastic machines of Jules Verne and boys' magazines. One of the British magazines used to show on its pictorial covers the vehicles in which the hero, Frank Reade, crossed deserts and smashed his way through jungles, despite the interference of the technologically less advanced natives. The machines were steam-driven with spiked wheels for cross-country grip; at the front they had searchlights and elephant-sized cow-catchers, and they bristled with cannon and quick-firers. Their armour was angular and rivetted. Bizarre though they were, reality in the end outdid them.

Opposite: a post-war French souvenir inkwell (for ink, lift the manhole cover in no-man's-land).

This page: hours of boredom were occupied making representations of the guns which produced mass barrages on a scale the world had never seen (or heard) before. *Top:* brass guns, some with wheels and barrels made from shell-caps or cartridges. *Upper middle:* a long-range railway gun model, which could fire a .22 cartridge and kill someone in the next suburb. *Lower middle:* a most elegant brass gun. *Bottom:* a sober, serviceable and extremely heavy German specimen in cast iron, stove-blacked.

WILLS'S CIGARETTES.

ARMOURED CARS.

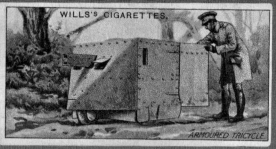

WILLS'S CIGARETTES.

ARMOURED TRICYCLE.

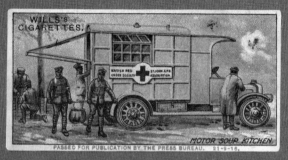

WILLS'S CIGARETTES.

MOTOR SOUP KITCHEN.

PASSED FOR PUBLICATION BY THE PRESS BUREAU. 21-9-16.

WILLS'S CIGARETTES.

MOTOR PIGEON-COTE.

WILLS'S CIGARETTES.

MOTOR MACHINE GUN BATTERY.

WILLS'S CIGARETTES.

MOTOR WIRE CUTTER.

However, the armoured cars were plainly not going to solve the deadlock of trench warfare. The real excitement was therefore reserved for the arrival of the tank, which clearly could do just that.

As soon as the official announcements were released (without, for some time, any pictures), everyone thought he knew exactly what tanks were going to be like, and cartoonists and postcard artists rushed to the drawing board. At first nobody realized that they were tracked vehicles, and even this information got out before any details of their precise shape were released. The Germans who actually saw them presumably reported straight back to Berlin, but a decent interval was allowed to elapse for everyone on the Allied home fronts to get thoroughly confused.

Once the clear simple lozenge shape appeared in officially released photographs, the tank became an immensely popular image to the Allies. It was new, it was going to change the face of war, it was going to win the war. This enthusiasm remained undimmed though the tanks achieved little for over a year; even when properly used at Cambrai, in September 1917, it was without effective support so that the battle as a whole was a flop. However, the faith with which they were greeted was in the end justified (as Ludendorf later testified); they were a major factor in breaking the stalemate, and they did change the face of war.

Their popularity is demonstrated by the fact that, of all the hand-made souvenirs we have found, there are more representing tanks than any other weapon or image of war, and the Crest industry made more versions of the tank than of anything else.

The basic steel lozenge of the British tank was translated into a remarkable variety of forms. Angular or rounded, dumpy or elongated, hump-backed, tall or short, they were made both plain and fancy. They were churned out by do-it-yourselfers and by industry in brass, copper lead, aluminium, silver-plate, tin-plate, wood and china, and even in bone in the manner of French prisoner of war work in the Napoleonic wars.

Left: technology very soon caught up with even the weirdest devices illustrated in pre-war boys' magazines, as can be seen from this selection of armoured vehicles from a set of Wills's Cigarette cards of 1916.

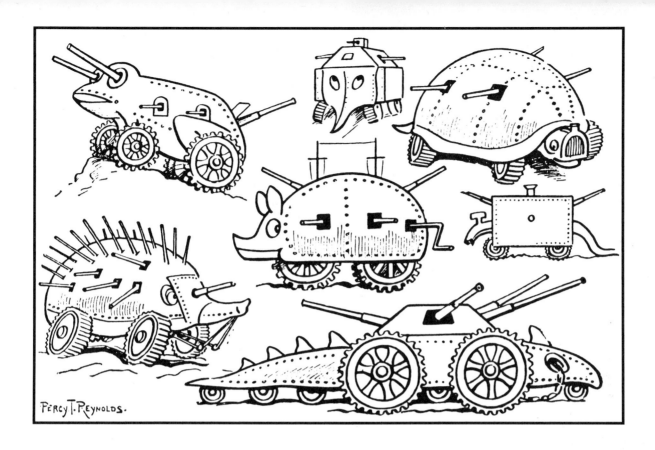

When the first news of the tanks was released in Britain (without, for some time, any pictures), comic artists rushed to the drawing board to produce their own interpretations of this new marvel. *Top: Punch*'s selection. *Left:* Heath Robinson's version. *Right:* a postcard.

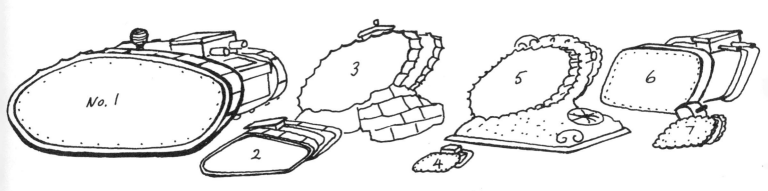

Some useful tanks. The tank was an ideal shape for a fanciful container. All these versions were based on the lozenge-shaped British tank, shown for comparison bottom right; the variety is a great tribute to the inventive and interpretative powers of the popular imagination. (1) Jewel box with seven drawers—some very secret; wood with inlaid brass flowers and a George V penny let into the back. (2) Watch-holder, inscribed 'Amiens' and 'Gertie'. (3) and (5) Inkwells; brass castings. (4) Advertisement paper-weight; gun-metal. (6) Money-box; sheet brass on wood, with brass carpet-nails for rivets. (7) and (12) Cigarette lighters (lift the turret); aluminium. (8) and (9) Money-boxes; wood. (10) Collecting money-box; china. (11) Pin-cushion; silver plate. (13) Whistle. (14) 'Monopoly' piece.

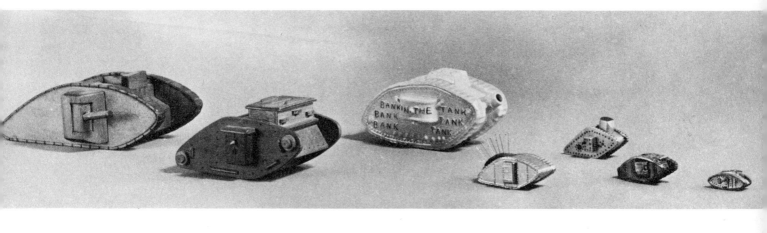

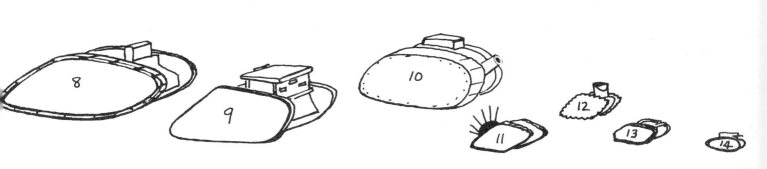

A very long, thin money-box with ebony trim.

When the first tanks were dispatched to the front by rail, they were still secret, so they had to be swaddled from the gaze of rumour-mongers and spies. In order to offer some explanation as to what these gigantic parcels contained, they were code-named 'Tanks' and the name stuck. As this apt pseudonym suggests, tanks are containers, and as such could be adapted to many domestic roles. It was the money-box aspect which was exploited in the 'Bank in the Tank' campaign in Britain to raise money for the war effort. Tanks back from France toured the cities of Britain, mayors mounted them and made speeches, model tanks were handed round as collecting boxes (there is a beautiful one made of matchsticks in the Tank Museum at Bovington). A British tank later toured the United States, and waddled down Broadway.

The greatest difficulty with model tanks was to make them go along. The technology of the caterpillar track was causing enough headaches among the armaments designers; it proved quite beyond the ingenuity of the amateur model makers. So the hand-made models were usually static ornaments; those that could move did so on wheels, sometimes added furtively, sometimes quite shamelessly. True mobility did not come until the post-war boom in clockwork versions, mostly from Germany. (We have an unconfirmed report that prisoners of war used to conduct races with mouse-powered tanks, but we haven't yet managed to find one.)

The German High Command had been caught napping by the development of the tank and were slow and hesitant in their response. One large, ponderous affair was designed, but by the Armistice only a handful had been produced. Little wonder, then, that when the German toy industry returned to peaceful production, it was Allied models that were turned out, chiefly British ones—there was, after all, a good market in Britain.

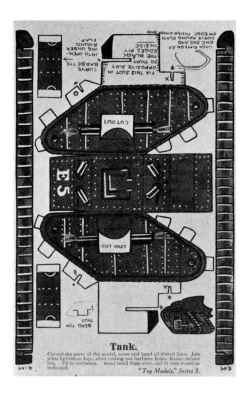

Left top: A brass money-box. *Left middle:* a charming black wooden money-box, hunched up like a mole; the designer has evaded the problem of devising tracks for a simple toy, and has used cast-iron wheels, quite serviceable enough for the terrain of the nursery floor. *Left bottom:* surely the maddest of them all. The tracks are bicycle chains, rigidly fixed, and it runs on roller-skate wheels; the device on top defies interpretation. *Right top:* a cut-out tank on a postcard. *Right middle:* a soap tank for cleaning up the enemy. *Right bottom:* a post-war nursery 'tank' made from a cotton reel, a rubber band, a candle end and a matchstick; it grinds along exceedingly slowly and will climb a very small obstacle.

As a toy, the tank was a winner. Like the toy cannon it could actually participate in the battle; it could climb obstacles, flatten enemy infantry, its gun could fire (or at any rate emit sparks), and its commander could be made to pop his head out of the turret. A dramatic and satisfying toy.

Like the model makers, some toy manufacturers were defeated by the caterpillar track, and resorted to wheels; however, others found a solution in rubber tracks, and some contrived successful and realistic interlocking metal ones; there are very small models with square-link chain. One German-made lozenge-shaped tank with rubber tracks exploited the diagonal symmetry of the basic form so that if in attempting to climb an obstacle it toppled over on its back, there it was, the same old lozenge, trying again and again. Heaven knows what was supposed to happen to the crew.

Technological advance changed not only the face of the war, but also the face of the warrior. Ever since the medieval visor went out of fashion the face of the fighting man had been a human face, even though his body was distorted with frogging and epaulettes and his height increased by tall headgear. The advent of gas and gas masks meant a return to a caricaturing of the human visage that went beyond the wildest nightmares of the Surrealists. This was the only major war in which gas was used, and though gas masks were carried in the Second World War they did not figure much in popular imagery.

The entire image of the fighting man changed. By 1915 the armies of all nations were wearing various shades of drab, though the French spurned giving up all trace of their traditional blue. Armoured headgear returned, so that by 1916 the soldier's image had been altered out of all recognition.

Above: 'The Evolution of the Fighting Man' from 'Canada in Khaki'. *Opposite:* The advent of gas changed the face of the fighting man, and produced a whole series of new bogey-man images, soon picked up by the illustrators and cartoonists, as on this cover of *La Baïonnette*. No one produced anything weirder than the actual objects, a selection of which is shown alongside.

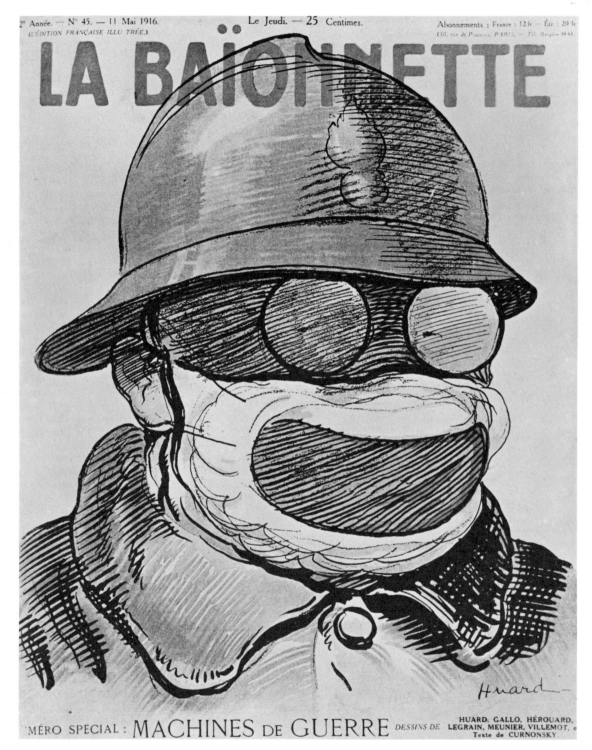

Camouflage was an entertaining new phenomenon. *Far left:* Bairnsfather saw the hazards of over-elaborate camouflage gear. *Left:* model of an actual dummy tree displayed soon after the war at the Imperial War Museum, London, but not, alas, to-day. *Above:* Australian troops carry a canvas spoof tank. *Below:* an imitation dead horse to hide a man with his ear to the ground. *Bottom right:* how a French cartoonist saw the spying potential of the fake tree.

Opposite: cartoonists were quick to see the comic possibilities of things not seeming what they were, which even gave the opportunity for a mild anti-Semitic joke.

Camouflage!

Say. kid! if that aint camouflage. ask me what is!

Camouflage was another new phenomenon that produced a complete new visual language —and a new breed of jokes. By some uncharacteristic act of imagination, the Allied forces brought in professional artists to tackle this problem of visual sleight-of-hand. The most important new idea they produced was that of disguising an object by means of a superimposed pattern in contrasting colours which confused the underlying form (at sea they went even further and produced something called dazzle camouflage). Considering that most of the artists involved were of academic outlook, some of the results they produced are astonishing. They often succeeded in out-cubing the Cubists, sometimes to the apparent detriment of the original objective.

The pretty uniforms and prancing horses of earlier wars had been displaced for ever by dirt-coloured men and speckled dirt-coloured machines. The popular artists were not dismayed, however; they loved the machines and decided that khaki was beautiful.

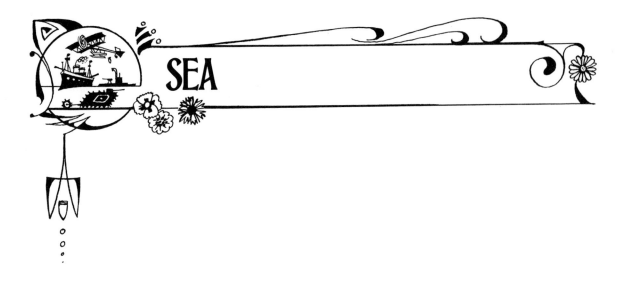

SEA

Sailors have always been active creators of popular art. They often have time on their hands, most have some degree of handicraft skill, and their vocation encourages them to be observant. Seafaring fills a man's mind with a wide variety of visual memories of different places and cultures, with a special corner reserved for the sights and thoughts of home. Homecoming demands presents, and what better than a token of hours spent thinking of absent ones?

There are, however, severe limitations to a sailor's creative endeavours. In the days of hammock and ditty-bag, there was nowhere to keep large or delicate artworks so those afloat tended to be restricted to small carvings and solid models. There was little opportunity to go in for ship models with elaborate rigging and glass cases.

The shore-based, the retired, the captive and the convalescent suffered no such limitations, and later there were the demobilized with memories to immortalize for the mantel-shelf. Their products vary in intention and achievement; some are expert jobs well up to the standard of dockyard scale models, others are highly fanciful or just plain inaccurate.

The Dreadnoughts furnished an image of sea power which gripped the imagination of nations and individuals. They stirred Winston Churchill to a passage of prose purple even for him, with metaphors mixed to fine effect:

'We may now picture this great fleet, with its flotillas and cruisers, steaming out of Portland Harbour, squadron by squadron, scores of gigantic castles of steel wending their way across the misty shining sea, like giants bowed in anxious thought.'
(The Passage of the Grand Fleet through the Straits of Dover, 29 July, 1914, from *The World Crisis*.)

Manufacturers in every country continued to pour out, as they had for decades, clock-work and steam battleships that floated, little lead ones that didn't, and flotillas of wooden waterline models for table-top battles. Dread-noughts were featured on calendars, in boys' magazine illustrations and on postcards.

Opposite: ship models are usually to scale and hence lack artistic invention. Not so this one, however, which vividly captures the spirit of the great ironclads.

A dashing little British model of HMS *Neptune*, signed Charles Ashley, 1916. Sailors hand-in-hand line the rails, officers man their stations and foam splashes along the sides.

The Great War saw the promotion of the submarine from a rather ungentlemanly freak to a highly ungentlemanly potential war-winner. (Before the war in the Royal Navy submariners had been referred to as 'dirty little men in dirty little boats'.) After Jutland, the submarine was the dominant factor in naval warfare and as a result frequently featured in propaganda cartoons and posters. Toy manufacturers perfected the technology of bathtub submersion and clockwork submarines had a long run of popularity. Makers of hand-made brass models favoured the submarine, as the lack of rigging and external fuss gave it a high survival rate when subjected to the hazards of being packed away half-made, or sent home by post.

Embroidery was not held to be in any way unmanly in the Royal Navy, and flourished. Swags of Allied flags were much favoured (Britain usually represented by the White Ensign) flanking a photograph of a group of shipmates framed in a fancy border. The needlework was usually in wool or mercerized cotton, often on a navy blue background. Sometimes there was an anchor or a ship included in the design and almost always dates and a location: 'Souvenir of the China Station 1914–1915', 'Gibraltar 1917–1919', etc. When it was safely at home, it was stretched and put in an oak frame. Pictures of ships or shipmates were sometimes put in frames shaped like lifebelts, with *HMS Pinafore,* or whatever, lettered round and usually a flag or two.

Since postcards were such an appropriate means of communication between traveller and home (and vice versa), sailors and their families formed a special market for them. There are many sailors' dreams of Home and Beauty featured in tinted sepia and fond messages framed in flowers and flags from Mum and Dad to Our Boy in Blue.

Top: a French nautical postcard. *Bottom:* French cut-out sailors and ship.

Gott-strafe England

The immense range of Great War naval gunnery spoiled the fun for painters of naval battles, as the two sides were miles apart. The official painters cheated a bit, the popular artists like mad, but the artist of the painting above didn't have to cheat at all—the poor old *Aboukir*, *Hogue* and *Cressy* really were about that far apart when they were torpedoed by the U9. *Left middle:* a German postcard shows cruisers bombarding the British coast. *Bottom left:* a British view of German naval activity. *Bottom right:* a brass submarine made from rifle bullets.

THE GERMAN NAVY TAKING ROOT!

STIKPHASTZ

AND THE GREEN GRASS GREW ALL ROUND ME BOYS!

The sea war in Crest china.

Postcard designers found themselves confronted with the problem that has faced naval artists since the arrival of high-velocity guns: modern sea battles are fought at such a range that you can't get both sides into the same picture without the ships becoming microscopic. Attempts to get over this problem led to some dramatic and highly fanciful results.

The sea war was also popular with the Crest designers. They made warships galore—capital ships, cruisers, destroyers, submarines and minesweepers; several varieties of mine, a torpedo and a naval gun. There was no lack of evidence on which to base their models (the warship was a favourite postcard subject, and there was always *Jane's Fighting Ships*), so the dotty effects sometimes produced can either be put down to acts of imagination or to just not bothering. For instance, though there is one quite convincing model of the *Queen Elizabeth*, there are several odd efforts, in-cluding one with three funnels (she only had two); the same model also appeared bearing the name HMS *Tiger*. There is a two-fun-nelled hospital ship called HMHS *Anglia*, but the same lettering also appears on a four-funnelled model; this latter in turn appears, without the red cross, called *Lusitania*, and finally there is a good scale model *Lusitania*, correctly named. One charming and comical feature of the warship models is that their gun turrets have pairs of guns diverging at about twenty degrees. Perhaps the designers were misled by those dramatic pictures taken from deck level of great pairs of barrels soaring into the sky, raking up from the turret in steep perspective (often with a ship's boy or the ship's cat sticking out of the barrel). These models suggest a new concept of naval gunnery where, by adroit manoeuvering, it would be possible to score a left and a right, and sink two enemy ships with the same salvo.

This page: a German cartoon of King George V and Queen Mary at breakfast soon after the loss of Kitchener on HMS *Hampshire*. The caption reads 'King George V, on receiving news of Kitchener's death was shocked to the marrow. His first comment was, "Oh! In that case we can't eat any more fish from the North Sea".'

Opposite: another cartoon from *Simplicissimus* entitled 'Wilson's Dream'.

German officers on leave relax on a boating pond. Come in, U9!

The long-expected clash between the great battle fleets of Britain and Germany came and went in May 1916 in fitful mist and finally in failing light, remote, impossible to photograph. Both sides claimed a victory. In Britain at least there were a few sceptics. Even Admiral Beatty said, 'There's something wrong with our bloody ships.' Jellicoe, the British Commander in Chief, had the awful responsibility of being the only man on either side who could lose the war in an afternoon. But despite heavy British losses, after the battle the German fleet effectively stayed in port till it came out to surrender; a baffling anti-climax, which perhaps accounts for the decline of popular interest in the navies that seems to have occurred in the last years of the war.

The submarine war dominated the scene from then on. Gallant U-boat commanders figured on decorative German armbands sold to raise money for the war; accounts of convoys, Q-ships and the sinking of merchant shipping filled the Allied press.

The war at sea, like the war on land, hadn't turned out a bit as everyone had expected.

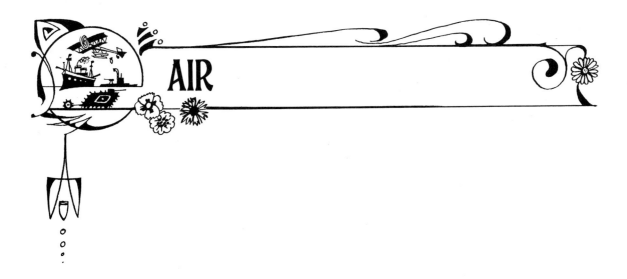

AIR

There had been wars on land and wars at sea ever since history began, but never a war in the air, except in the stories of the prophetic romancers and they got it hopelessly wrong. Even H. G. Wells, whose visions were nearest the mark, saw aerial combat, in his *Sleeper Awakes*, in terms of ramming—if his aircraft failed first time they went round again and had another go. In a rare lapse from his usually sound technological intuition, he failed to see that a collision which wrecked one combatant would tear both to pieces—as in fact sometimes happened. On this basis, each combat would be a one-all draw; it almost certainly meant the suicide of the attacking crew. This approach did not commend itself to airmen, nor, oddly enough in a war noted for a spendthrift attitude to human life and a widespread philosophy of attrition, to the High Commands. Perhaps it was because aircraft were so expensive.

Aerial combat began in a fairly sporting way with airmen firing pistols at each other, tossing hand grenades and even bricks; rifles and duck guns were used. Success was rare.

Images of aerial warfare soon appeared on postcards, sometimes depicting these primitive combats, sometimes flights over enemy cities, another new dimension to war. A Zeppelin engaged in such a flight was intercepted by Sub-Lieutenant Warneford, on 7 June 1915; he dropped small bombs on it till it exploded—a rare victory for air-to-air bombing (from then on, the machine gun was the dominant weapon). Warneford's exploit caught the British public's imagination and was immediately celebrated on picture postcards. Stories of later victories over airships were told on sets of postcards (*The Arrival, Danger Ahead, Nearing Disaster, Airman Attacks, Well Alight, Nearing the End, Final Rapid Fall*; another series ends *An Incandescent Mass—Finis*). Some claimed to be based on 'an eye-witness account', 'an onlooker's sketch'; some, by evasive captioning, implied that they were actual photographs. Coloured cards of flaming Zeppelins were gleefully titled *A Nasty Jar for the Baby-Killers, The Finest Sight I Ever Saw, Hot Stuff*. One caption quoted a German claim to have bombed 'a huge shell factory': the picture shows a bomb bursting in a hencoop.

Aeroplanes and airships were already part of the stock-in-trade of the popular artist,

L. HINGRE

311

Aerial warfare provided plent
of new images for the popula
arts. *Left:* a French aeria
battlescape from the pistol
and-brickbat era of air comba
Opposite: a fretwork desig
from *Hobbies* weekly.

as balloons had been before them. Pre-war Christmas cards showed Santa Claus arriving in a primitive aircraft laden with parcels. Greeting cards bore floral aircraft; a popular British seaside card was a photograph of the whole family crammed into a canvas-and-paint Bleriot monoplane, all looking rather solemn and uncomfortable. Comic cards showed elephants on flimsy aircraft, hundreds of babies arriving in decorative ones, and jokes about people falling out of them (as this was a rare occurrence pre-war, it was still acceptable as a comic idea; it went out of favour when young men took to jumping out without parachutes rather than face a hideous death by burning as their planes spun down).

The Zeppelin had caught the public fancy in pre-war Germany. These were the closing years of the great period of the German post-card industry (it was never the same after the war), but in the Zeppelin cards all its best qualities are still there—the superb printing (often in chromolithography), the wonderful instinct for closely-packed design, the wild fantasy—flying fishes bearing gondolas, airships made of forget-me-nots, babies sitting astride green and gold Zeppelins.

At Friedrichshafen, the home of the Zeppelins, you could buy a very chubby china airship ashtray, with an indentation along the top for the ash, suitable for the cigars that Germans were always smoking in Allied cartoons. European manufacturers, mainly in Germany, had for years been producing tin-plate toys, lead toys and larger clockwork toys based on flying machines of all types. Many are fantasies, but scarcely more weird than some of the things that people tried to fly—and sometimes actually did.

Manufacturers soon adapted to the war. The flying babies on the postcards adopted military headgear and hurled bombs. The Allies seized on the Zeppelin as a symbol of German barbarity and soon made the visual pun of relating it to the national sausage. Airships were shown with the Kaiser's face on the front end, and the decline of Germany was symbolized by the detumescent Zeppelin.

The aeroplane became a favourite with the sparetime brass-smiths. Shell cases were flattened to provide thin plate for wings; rifle bullets became fuselages and wheels were made from sawn-off butt-ends of cartridges, tunic buttons, small coins. The cult of making these little souvenir planes was widespread, perhaps on both sides of no-man's-land, though this is hard to tell. There is so much fanciful invention that it is usually impossible to say which nation's machine is being depicted, and even when it is obvious you still can't tell who made it. One German Taube is made of a British bullet, with British buttons for wheels—Tommy depicting familiar enemy plane, or Fritz using Allied *objets trouvés?* Many have German crosses on the wings (sometimes in another metal, sometimes incised), but this does not prove German origin, as one of them has on its top wing 'World War —France' written in English. The one illustrated on page 9, however, must surely be German, as the decoration between the Maltese crosses consists of marguerites (the German soldiers' emblem). This is unlikely to have come from the hand of an Allied soldier.

Opposite: air heroes figure in two German advertisements (Leibniz cakes are good for you at high altitude), but the cheerful little French cut-out aviator seems to have that extra ingredient.

Flieger

Georgi. 15.

Feist Feldgrau
im Felde

CARL TIPS KARLS RUHE

Feist-Sektkellerei A.G. Frankfurt a.M.

TYPES DE GUERRE
L'AS
THE ACE

The amateur brass-smith used great ingenuity in transforming rifle cartridges into fuselages. Sometimes an extra bullet was soldered onto the butt-end to elongate it, sometimes a heavy machine gun cartridge was used for a larger model. Bullets were used in one example for the seven cylinders of a rotary engine (the correct number for the French Gnome engine, which powered many Allied aircraft).

Struts, wire bracing, undercarriages, all gave opportunities for ingenuity, invention and elaboration. Allied roundels were indicated by incised circles, sometimes coloured in. Makers of three-dimensional popular art excel in seeing and exploiting visual parallels —a date-box can become a tank, a button, a wheel. Some of the plane makers made little rotary engines with grub-screws to represent cylinders—the kind of visual pun later exploited in Meccano designs.

Not all examples have cartridges for fuselages, and not all are made of brass—copper and aluminium were also used. Some were given a rather amateur nickel-plated finish. Although with the passing years this has acquired a rather attractive grotty patina, it does tend to obscure the nature of the assembled materials—indeed, on the unplated models the contrast between soldered joints and bare brass is part of the character, as in good quality plumbing work.

Such models were strictly for the mantelshelf and were quite unsuitable for ham-fisted children whose zooming and rat-tat-tatting dog-fights demanded something chunkier in wood; specimens have survived. Similar wooden ones were made as weather-vanes, usually mounted on potting sheds in allotments or gardens, with little propellers that blew round in the wind to scare the birds.

The air war provided lots of material for the Crest manufacturers. Before the war they had made models of balloons and Bleriot-type monoplanes; some of the latter are marked *Model of Army Aeroplane*, wording which rather suggests a pre-war date. However, some specimens have red, white and blue British roundels, a form of identification not introduced until 1915; these must be of wartime vintage. Other monoplane models followed. One type had wings patterned like moss and a circular blob like a banjo behind the cockpit to carry the crest. It appears in various sizes some with two-, some with three-bladed propellers.

In the Bleriot models the wheels were attached direct to the narrow fuselage, making it an unstable ornament; later types solved this problem by having the wheels on stalks which were attached halfway along each wing. This sensible idea was well ahead of its time —it anticipated the Hurricane by twenty-five years.

The problem of modelling in china such fine features as undercarriages and struts led to some comical distortions and over-simplifications—the conflict between form and materials that has faced sculptors throughout history. When it came to biplanes, some designers ducked the problem altogether and filled the space between the wings with a solid lump on which they marked the struts. Some made separate wings joined by one simple fat strut faired into the wing at either end; this looks like nothing more than an expedient convention for the china modeller, but there was in fact a British experimental aircraft, the SE4, with struts of exactly this type. Only one was built, and it never went to France, but it got some publicity in early 1914 when it flew at the then remarkable speed of 135 mph.

Opposite: brass aeroplanes, the fuselages made from cartridges. The triplane (nickel-plated) appears to be a wild fantasy, but take a look some time at the FIAT CA4; apart from the latter's twin tail booms, this is it. The oriental monoplane has Egyptian coins on its wings as roundels.

Top left: brass biplane with an interesting but unlikely strutting system. *Top right:* an acorn and sycamore-seed monoplane made by Belgian soldiers and sold to raise money. *Middle right:* a brass parasol monoplane with a rotary engine with bullets for cylinders. *Bottom:* if this aircraft had ever really existed, it should surely have been called the Bristol Bassethound; thick and chap-fallen, it looks, and is, totally ground-bound. A primitive electric motor drives the airscrew, but not enough even to make it taxi. Though more or less based on the British SE5, it has French markings.

Opposite: a fretwork biplane epergne; the raised roundels were to support three small vases.

94

Later a bolder spirit at the Arcadian Works in Stoke-on-Trent modelled a large Crest biplane with separated wings and a convincing set of struts—a considerable feat of modelling and china firing.

Airships were an easier shape to make in china, though the British Army airship 'Beta' presented problems, its gondola being slung below the envelope on wires. The solution was to show the group of wires as appliquéd lines on a solid triangle. The Zeppelin made a perfect subject; it was one of the few enemy objects depicted in Crest. These models were, of course, celebrating Allied successes in shooting down raiders. One example, with a vast propeller attached to its stern, bears the legend 'Zeppelin destroyed by Lieut. Leefe-Robinson VC at Cuffley, Essex, Sept 3, 1916'. Another marked 'L33' is a good representation of the one which was damaged by gunfire over London on 14 September 1916 and was then attacked by an aircraft. It came down at Wigborough, Essex, where its crew surrendered to a bewildered special constable.

The bombs that fell from Zeppelins were also modelled, with inscriptions telling where they fell—Sheringham, Maldon, Bury St Edmunds. Two of these are by W. H. Goss and depict the type of incendiary bomb used in early raids, consisting of a canister full of an inflammable solid mixture with resin-impregnated rope wound round the outside. Those that survived to be portrayed were, of course, duds, and some can be seen in the Imperial War Museum in London.

Zeppelins were also portrayed in desk-top ornaments, souvenirs and toys, and were the subject of endless postcard jokes. A Zeppelin over London featured on a British poster which said: IT IS FAR BETTER TO FACE THE BULLETS THAN TO BE KILLED AT HOME BY A BOMB—JOIN THE ARMY AT ONCE AND HELP STOP AN AIR RAID. That's not all you might have stopped.

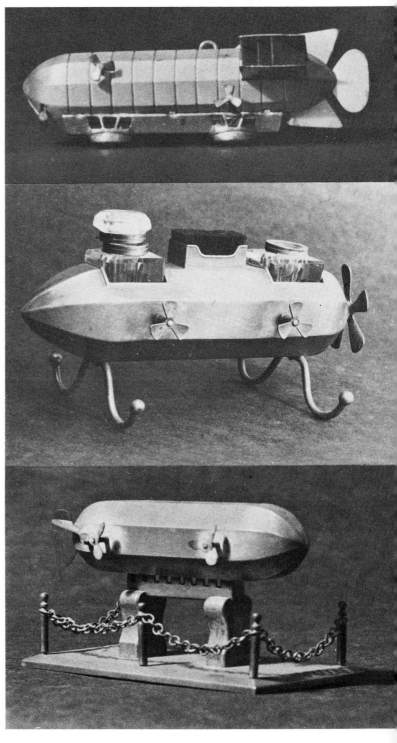

Opposite: the air war in Crest china. Under the Zeppelins, German bombs; at the bottom, ANTI ZEPPELIN CANDLESTICK, a weapon which must have struck terror into the German aircrews. The tractor is a type used to pull aircraft about airfields. The airman is holding a small box—perhaps he is modelled on a newspaper photograph of a hero leaving Buckingham Palace holding his medal. *This page. Top:* a Zeppelin tape measure. *Middle:* an inkwell and penwiper. *Bottom:* a charming and useless Zeppelin monument. As with the tape measure, good for sideways travel—take a look at the propellers.

A French theatre poster. Oh to have seen that show! *Bottom:* a German cartoon shows a British baby kept so long in a London cellar by the Zeppelin raids that it has broken out in mushrooms.

98

Sale Aviatik!
Qu'est-ce qu'il te met le loustic.

THE V.C "ZEP" WRECKER.
Flight Sub-Lieutenant R.A.J. Warneford.
who destroyed a Zeppelin with bombs at a
height of 6,000 ft. The Explosion caused his
machine to turn upside down, but he righted
himself and landed in enemy country, escaped.
but was killed a fortnight later while
testing a new Aeroplane near Paris.

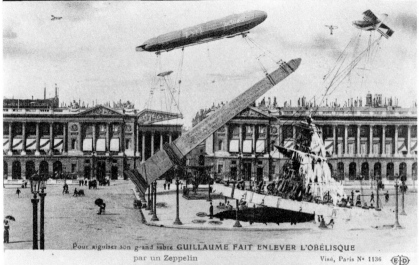

Pour aiguiser son grand sabre GUILLAUME FAIT ENLEVER L'OBÉLISQUE
par un Zeppelin   Visé, Paris Nº 1136

Deutscher Flieger über Paris

Left. Top: heroic French infant bombs German aircraft. *Middle:* this British card was issued within days of Warneford's victory over the LZ37. When he was killed a few days later, the manufacturers pasted on an additional strip of paper below the caption to complete the story. *Bottom:* a German card showing a Taube over the Eiffel Tower scattering bombs; issued by the 'German Airfleet Union for the Creation of a Strong German Airfleet and for the furthering of Air Training.' *Right. Top:* in order to get space for the sender's portrait, the propeller of this Bleriot monoplane has been moved to the rear, an arrangement often favoured in toys of this period. *Bottom:* a French vision of German baseness. The ladies with umbrellas aren't too worried.

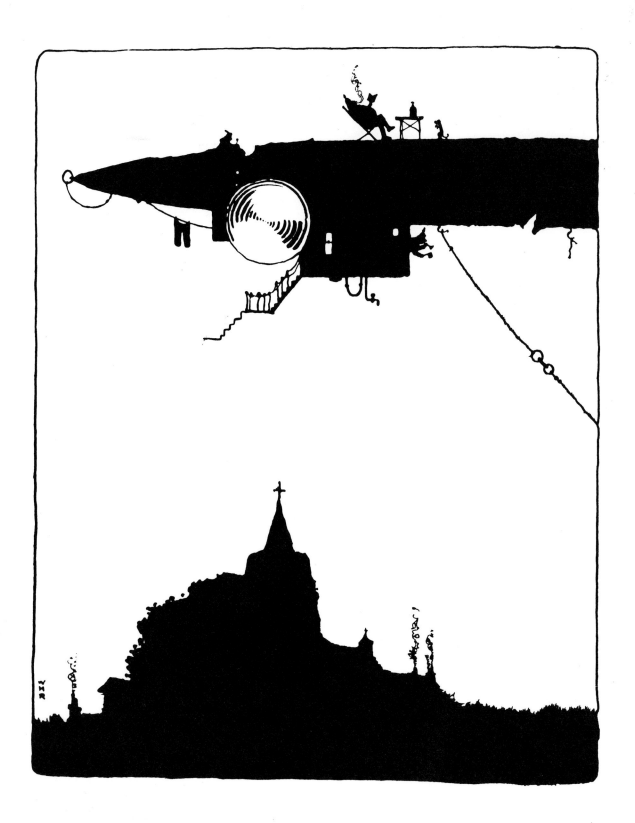

From Heath Robinson's *The Saintly Hun* captioned 'Love of children.
Old dears in a *Shütte Lanz* taking a peasant's child for a little run.'

Left: a strictly post-war image for the British, who allowed no such softness in wartime. *Above:* dog-fight in brasswork.

The little parachutist opposite is wearing RAF blue and pilot's goggles. Even if we didn't know it from the lady who made him, the parachute tells us he was a post-war flier, for British wartime pilots were not issued with them. A workable design existed, and was used in a crude form in observation balloons, but some appalling mental blockage decided the authorities against issuing them. Some thought pilots might bail out prematurely; others perhaps thought that rather than be entrusted to such a relatively untried device, the boys might as well be left to fry.

The Germans, who towards the end were fighting a defensive air war, had more to gain, as their pilots would usually land on their own side of the lines, and they were using parachutes by 1918. (One who survived was Ernst Udet, who later helped Goering to build up the Luftwaffe.) The wasteful British attitude is odd considering both the value to the war effort of experienced pilots and the adulation with which airmen were regarded by the public. Fighter pilots especially were celebrated and hero-worshipped. Most schoolboys even today, could name a handful of Great War fliers, and they would all be fighter pilots. Who knows by name one bomber or reconnaissance pilot, let alone an observer? Unknown warriors indeed.

All nations were gripped by the glamour of these latter-day knights, who killed each other decently far above the mud. For Germans, the reburial of von Richthofen in Berlin after the war was their equivalent of the Unknown Soldier ceremonies in other countries. His memory lives on on both sides of the Atlantic in *Snoopy and the Red Baron.*

The top decorations tended to go to fighter pilots; in contrast, in the Second World War, only one of the VCs given to the RAF went to Fighter Command. There were many reasons for this, but one was a deliberate attempt to glamorize Bomber Command. Just as well; they were after all the cannon-fodder of their war.

PARCELS & POST

When Tommy used to be at home,
He'd often treat the wenches,
So now the Girls send Goodies out
To Tommy in the Trenches.

The picture above this verse on the postcard shows two rosy-cheeked little girls in short frills, socks and ribbons, carrying piles of neat, apparently feather-weight parcels. They are bouncing along to the post office and their beribboned puppy dog is bouncing with them. Later we shall be looking at children in wartime in more detail; meanwhile these symbolize the light-hearted popular vision of the goodies and comforts that flowed from home to the front.

All the nations involved made great efforts to deliver parcels to all the more accessible fronts (letters and postcards went everywhere), and the Red Cross organizations managed to get a great many parcels to prisoners of war. The difficulties lay with the sender—what goodies to send, how packed, how perishable, how heavy? What *did* they need? Thousands had no serving friends or relations, but they made up parcels just the same, to go to a local contingent or just into the blue to anyone.

At the beginning there was food—chocolates, home-made cakes, pots of jam—but as food became scarcer and dearer, such parcels became difficult except for the rich. Smokes, though remained possible; tobacco and pipes, cigarettes, or the little patent rollers with packets of thin paper for making them, were bound to be always welcome because a non-smoker could swop them for something else.

But better than something bought was something made, and what better than something to keep a soldier warm? Knitting became a craze; it had the great advantage that when parcels were sent to strangers of unknown size the products might stretch to fit. Balaclava helmets, mufflers, gloves, mittens, body-belts, knee-bands and socks, and socks, and socks, were knitted by the million. Unfortunately, the interesting trick by which one long thread of wool becomes a 3-D garment is not as simple as it looks—tension, size of needle, type of wool, must all be just right, and though such instructions as K1 P2 are easy enough to learn, rows must be counted and accuracy maintained. A lot of socks were used to polish boots.

Opposite: dream postcards from Britain, Austro-Hungary and Germany.

Industry soon came to the rescue of the parcel-senders with little novelties—fusées (impregnated yellow cotton ropes that smouldered away for pipe-lighting in trenches), pocket periscopes, metal lattice watch-guards, bullet-proof vests to protect the absent one, compressed food and malted-milk tablets, patent penknives and photoframes with mica fronts that gradually clouded. There were pens and stylos and writing compendiums to encourage letters home, and ingenious multi-purpose eating-and-shaving kits. The old advertisements and the memories of the senders are all that now remain of most of them.

One gift in particular was widely cherished by British soldiers. Princess Mary's brass gift box, beautifully designed by the architect Professor S. D. Adshead, went to every smoker at the front, filled with cigarettes and tobacco (non-smokers got a dreary little satchel of writing paper) in time for Christmas 1914—a triumph of organization that still makes us gasp. The boxes were well made

and thousands of them were kept intact. They can still be found with contents inviolate, and even put in frames.

Christmas was the most nostalgic time for everyone, and the two-way dream balloons illustrated on this page went everywhere with inscriptions in every language. These three are typical of thousands—there seem to be no cheerful ones, all are sad and most are sepia.

All through the war years the French postcard industry supplied British soldiers with lovely cards to send back in thanks for the parcels. There were sprays of real flowers and grasses, tied to the card with tricolour ribbon, and muslin cards embroidered in silks with regimental crests, the New Year's date in Allied flags, or Good Luck messages and symbols. Some had pockets enclosing tiny cards, *To my dear Mother*, etc. Embossed cardboard frames were glued over the edges of the muslin, and the cards were usually sent in envelopes; being small and easily stored, many have survived.

Protégez mon papa!

" —AND WATCH OVER MY DEAR DADDY."

Boldog karácsonyi ünnepeket!
E szent és csöndes éjszakán
Kitekintek a kaszárnya ablakán.
Szeretnek most hazamenni,
Édes szülém nálad lenni-holnapig.

Herzliche Weihnachtsgrüsse!

Am Wachtfeuer draußen ihr lieget,
Im Winter zur Weihnachtszeit,
Wir beten für euch, daß ihr sieget
Und ende des Krieges Leid.

Flowers of France

Gathered for you

OUVERT PAR LA CENSURE.

Top left: an elaborate French card with embroidered national flowers and dyed and silvered grasses. *Top right:* the seaside postcard style adapted to wartime needs. Many cards were captioned in both French and English, the translated jokes often being quite different from the original and usually pretty wide of the mark. Even cards of non-war subjects, like fluffy kittens, broke into bi-lingual captions, a brief postal *entente cordiale*. *Bottom right:* an Australian gift biscuit tin.

UNTIL (1).

No rose in all the world until you came,
No star until you smiled upon life's sea;
No song in all the world until you spoke,
No hope until you gave your heart to me.

UNTIL (2).

O rose, bloom ever in my lonely heart,
O star, shine steadfast with your light divine;
Ring on, O song, your melody of joy,
Life's crowned at last, and love, is ever mine.

Bamforth sets came in two, three or more cards, depending on the song.

The censorship regulations demanded that nothing from the front might carry an address, and that everything from home went to a number. But men evolved elaborate codes for conveying the meaningless name of some foreign village, so, to make censorship easier and more sure, the dull buff Field Service Post Card was introduced. It had stark sentences that could be struck out; nothing could be added, not even affectionate cryptograms like the British S.W.A.K.—Sealed With A Kiss; the cards were not popular. There were a lot of jokes about censorship, and there were joke Field Service Post Cards; real and joke cards are shown on page 110.

Another sort of censorship was imposed by illiteracy. Hundreds of cards say nothing more than 'Hoping this finds you as it leaves me in the pink xxx Your Fred'. But those at home in Britain could buy the postcards of Messrs Bamforth, and the words of popular songs carried the messages for them. Bamforths started as lantern-slide makers, using for models the family, employees and neighbours, posed before painted backgrounds. Later this technique was extended to sets of postcards, like that at the top of the page. There were hundreds of dull 'Official Photograph' cards published by the *Daily Mail*, but there were plenty of colourful imaginative cards of great victories, comic women, children, nurses, soldiers, Kaisers, John Bulls, dogs, cats and profiteers. Cards reflected every popular emotion—patriotism, heroism and plain boredom more surely than any other medium. They were cheap and quick to turn out as a vast industry already existed geared to the pre-war postcard boom.

FIX TO FIX TO
TOP OF BACK
WELT. OF HEEL
WELT (RIBBED) ALL SIZES 4in
4 SIZES FROM BACK OF HEEL TO TOE DECREASING.
FOOT (PLAIN)
REDUCE FOR TOE
SIZE I.
SIZE II.
SIZE III.
SIZE IV.
SIZE I.
×
SIZE II.
×
SIZE III.
×
SIZE IV.
×
LEG (PLAIN PART) ALL SIZES 8in
LEG
THIS SIDE
(× FOOT FINISHED)

SOCKMEASURE THE "M·I·K" SOCK-KNITTERS-HELP
MAN IN KHAKI.
DEAN LONDON

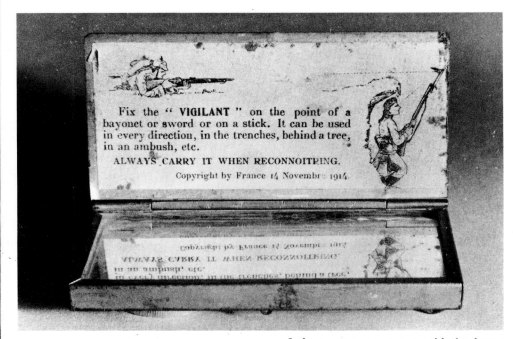

Fix the " VIGILANT " on the point of a
bayonet or sword or on a stick. It can be used
in every direction, in the trenches, behind a tree,
in an ambush, etc.
ALWAYS CARRY IT WHEN RECONNOITRING.
Copyright by France 14 Novembre 1914.

Left: a tape measure to aid the home
knitter. *Top:* a manufactured knick-knack
for Tommy's parcel.

Opposite. Left: a Russian Easter egg sold
to raise funds; a red cross on one side,
the Imperial monogram on the other.
Right: Princess Mary's gift tin sent to
every British smoker overseas for Christmas 1914, and an embroidered forces
greetings postcard.

NOTHING is to be written on this side except the date and signature of the sender. Sentences not required may be erased. If anything else is added the post card will be destroyed.

[Postage must be prepaid on any letter or post card addressed to the sender of this card.]

I am quite well.

I have been admitted into hospital
{ *sick* } *and am going on well.*
{ *wounded* } *and hope to be discharged soon.*

I am being sent down to the base.

I have received your { *letter dated* _____
{ *telegram „* _____
{ *parcel „* _____

Letter follows at first opportunity.

I have received no letter from you
{ *lately*
{ *for a long time.*

Signature
only }

Date _____

Wt. W1566-R1619-18539 8000m. 6-17. O. & Co., Grange Mills, S.W.

DATE ....

I have (not) received }
    your Letter dated } ....

I have been { Shopping.
              Flirting.
              Photographed.

I Love You { More than ever.
             Less than ever.
             Not at all.

Eats and Drinks are going slowly down.
                        —But not in Price.

I am in the Pink { Nightdress.
                    of Condition.

I think the War { this Year.
will end   next Year.
                 sometime.
                 never.

Someone has left you some money.
                        —I don't think

I write this { in Bed.
               at Home.
               on the Mat.

Letter follows soon as possible and wish I could
    come with it.

Strike out words   SIGNED ....
not required.   *Copyright 14-1-18.*

British official and unofficial postcards.

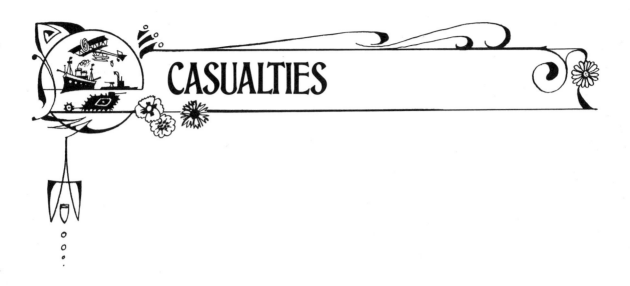

CASUALTIES

Today we are all familiar with the terrible and beautiful photographs of the Great War dead, rotting corpses, feet in boots, arms, skulls. They were not seen at the time. The first shattering exhibition in Britain was staged by the *Daily Express* in 1934. The display was simple, the photographs were large. One showed two lifesize men, torsos on metal legs, playing billiards. By comparison, the dead seemed lucky. There were rumours of much worse cases, men hardly alive, kept alive, never to be seen. After such revelations, war would have to stop. . . .

During the war, those at home saw or guessed little of this; the only corpses let through the censorship were enemy ones, and even they were usually fairly vague and out of focus. Few men who came back would ever talk about the war at all, at the time or afterwards. Their awful world was a closed book; with luck, even to themselves.

The popular arts created their own casualty world of bright hospital blue, and red crosses against stainless white, a charming world where bandages went becomingly round the head over a slight scalp wound and most bullets went in at the shoulder—what Siegfried Sassoon described as 'wounded in a mentionable place'. The Crest figures on page 114 show this world at its most naive— there is no horror or sadness in it, and the soldier isn't badly hurt. The figures are pretty ornaments, vehicles for the town crests just like the pre-war bathing machines and banjos.

But the war was not pretty. The front line, which in 1914 had meant 'a chance to get at 'em', was soon a stinking hell, and a 'blighty one' (a wound bad enough to mean repatriation, but not, it was hoped, mutilation) was often a more sensible dream than life itself. The stretcher became a palanquin, the hospital ship an Argo bound for home and the things soldiers made reflected this. In many fretwork ambulances, model stretcher parties and embroidered ships with red crosses on their sides, the convalescents expressed their appreciation and joy.

A reputedly true casualty story is that of the Indian wounded who were shipped back to England to a hospital set up in Brighton Pavilion, built by George IV in fantastic oriental style. Some of them woke from long periods of unconsciousness beneath its domes and thought themselves in heaven.

The fear of being maimed could always be balanced by the thought
that then, at any rate, you'd be out of it. These French realists are
saying to their passenger, you're lucky, mate, you've got a really nasty
one.

Opposite. Top: some amateur artists managed to carry their paints
and brushes through thick and thin; a gouache painting by Corporal
C. Goldspink (2nd Dragoon Guards) of No 14 Stationary Hospital
going up in flames. *Bottom:* an embroidered Belgian hospital ship.

Top: Crest china nurses with a very comfortable looking casualty, and to the right one of the lucky ones.
Left: a Hospital Blue pen-wiper.

Opposite: casualties, from the most tragic to the most trifling, were used to raise tears, laughs and funds. The nun and her Senegalese patient inform *La France* that they are her sentinels and that she may count on them.

"YOU'VE NOT SAID HOW I'VE GROWED, DADDY!"

From the painting by Thomas Henry

Hymne à la France

C'est nous tes sentinelles
France, compte sur nous.

102   H.M.T.

FIRST STEPS!

Première sortie.

BLINDED FOR YOU

Sold in aid of St. Dunstan's Hostel for Blinded Soldiers and Sailors

PRICE ONE PENNY.

Wars have always brought wounds and mutilation as well as death; they are expected and accepted. Partly because there is so much else of a human body to hit, and partly because heads and faces were often protected, blinding had been comparatively rare—what happened to King Harold at Hastings was a historic freak. The Great War brought gas, which burnt the eyes as well as the lungs, and introduced a new horror that no one tried to minimize. Some of the postcards on war-blindness are sickeningly, often embarrassingly, sentimental, but the fund-raising card on page 115 still hits us in a way that Sargeant's huge painting of a queue of blinded men never could.

There were other casualties, like prisoners of war who suffered a boredom worse than that of convalescence. There was no hope that tomorrow would be better than today. To while away the time they made elaborate objects, sometimes very touching ones. The Turkish prisoners did gorgeous beadwork, snakes, lizards, snakes swallowing lizards, and, of course, bead bags. The snakes have the date and 'Turkish Prisoner' in English on their bellies. Presumably they were made to sell to their captors who must have supplied the beads. The lizards are so small that there is only room on their bellies for the date.

"IS THERE A SOLDIER HERE WITH ONE LEG NAMED SMITH?"

"DUNNO, MUM — WHAT'S THE NAME OF HIS OTHER LEG?"

Above: the comic card maintained its heartless tradition.

Opposite: prisoners of war continued a great tradition of beautiful things made with simple materials that started with French prisoner work in the Napoleonic wars. This Turkish prisoner's snake is in white and amber beads with olive, prussian blue and scarlet patterns. The mouth is lined with crochet work. The aluminium box, elaborately incised with rococo patterns, is inscribed to 'Tittles' from Celle-Lager, a prison camp in Germany.

Thousands of buildings became casualties; whole villages and towns were reduced to piles of rubble or sank completely in the mud. The burning of the library at Louvain, the shelling of Rheims Cathedral were painted again and again, mostly by professional artists. Such picturesque scenes of destruction became very popular in coloured reproductions; few amateurs were inspired by fire or ruins, so the painting on page 112 is a rarity.

The ruins were amply recorded in photographs, though; every hamlet in northern France must have published its *Ruines de Tigeville* postcards, even if there was only a broken bridge to show. Although they were beautifully printed, and although the Anglo/ French captions are sometimes hilarious, they are the dullest cards of the war.

THE HOME FRONT

The popular arts on the home fronts of all countries on both sides point up the same problems and pleasures—hard (often unaccustomed) work, shortages and privations, balanced by a sense of participation with 'the boys'; the animal excitement and intimacy of war balanced by the sudden freezing presence of the enemy (Britain was lucky—only the bombs came; America was even luckier).

After the campaign to get the men, with its floods of recruiting posters, came the campaign to get the money. Having done what they could with taxes, governments exhorted civilians to match the sacrifices of the soldiers. There were simple, silly posters like the one on page 121, and also direct jabs below the belt: 'I gave my eyes—what have you given?' It was as impossible then as now to guess the ingredients of a successful poster. Maurice Rickards points out that the incredible American Red Cross image 'The Greatest Mother in the World', a monstrous damp figure of useless compassion, nursing a baby soldier on a baby stretcher, raised so much money that it was used again in the Second World War.

Every country had war bonds, which combined patriotism with a fixed percentage. Money was also raised for innumerable funds —for big charities under royal patronage or for local ones buying comforts for 'Our Boys'. Concerts were given by famous performers, with expensive seats and bright souvenir programmes, and there were bazaars selling garden produce, handicrafts, little manufactured objects and gifts from the gentry and local shops.

After the big money, there were still the pennies. Different countries had different ways of getting them—medallions, enamel badges, armbands and flag-days. People do like something for their money, and these little objects were all very pretty. The flags were mostly in the bright heraldic tradition, tiny strips of printed paper stuck round pins and worn in the coat. A penny or two was the normal sum to drop in the box, though more was hoped for, and sometimes there was an appeal to snobbery with a more elaborate, even a silk, token for sixpence or more.

Images of war penetrated the most traditional places in the most elegant disguises, such as the German cup and saucer on page 10. The more unlikely the juxtaposition of the martial or the patriotic with the practical, the better—Union Jack knickers on a pantomime dame, a bull-dog stamped on the butter, hats in the form of Imperial eagles made of real feathers.

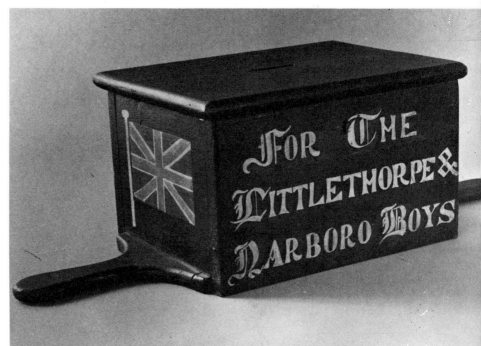

Left: a few of the colourful little paper flags fixed to pins to be stuck into the lapel to show that the wearer had given to the day's fund. *Top:* wooden collecting box made to raise money to buy comforts for the boys who went from Littlethorpe and Narborough in Leicestershire. *Above:* a metal fund-raising brooch sold in Germany.

Opposite page: Canadian war loan poster.

KEEP ALL CANADIANS BUSY

BUY 1918 VICTORY BONDS

Above: two views of a china gift bottle of Buchanan's whisky.

Opposite: war was no tea-party for those at the front, but at home tea-parties could be very warlike. On the left-hand table, a howitzer tea-pot, tank sugar-container, rifle toast-rack, shell tea-caddy, patriotic cup and saucer with Bleriot aeroplane inside cup, a hate tea-bell (surmounted by a skull in a *pickelhaube*) and a rosy paper napkin. The latter were sold in the streets of London for a penny. On the other table, an American field-gun cigarette lighter and an advertising ashtray (post-war, showing a new version of the jolly cad type of army officer). On the wall, a velvet-framed glass-painting commemorating the *Lusitania;* a water-colour of two apprehensive Allies; three happier Allies in Nottingham lace; and a food poster.

Hast du auch eine Fleischkarte, Mieze?

Top left: inkpot designed in the form of a loaf for the 'Save the Bread' campaign, July 1917. *Top right:* the little German girl asks her kitten if it too has a meat card. *Bottom left:* a wartime paper bag, one of a series of twenty-six which made up a complete Selfridge alphabet. What on earth were 'Wollies'? *Bottom right:* one of a series of six jolly postcards about food rationing.

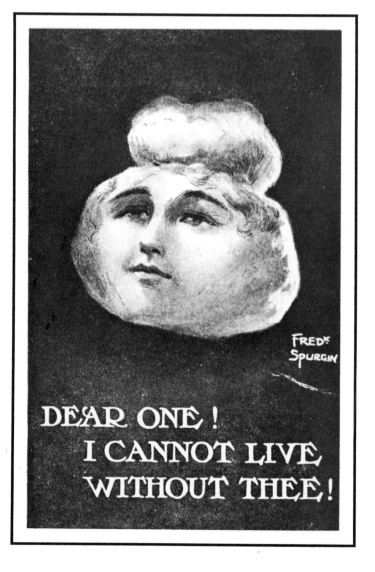

Tea pot: You're a deserter!
Tea: No I'm not, I'm only an absent-tea.

Hamster-Erlebnisse.   *Oh, meine Liebling*

Top right: the English pun continues to give pleasure. *Middle right:* A German policeman uncovers a hoarded ham. *Below left:* one staple food-stuff after another became scarce. *Below centre:* 'Marge' was better than no butter. *Below right:* substitute foods were better laughed about than groaned over.

Nobody bothers about me now like they used to— I wish I was lump sugar!

RISEN from the RANKS.

MARGARINE

Don't touch it, dear, it's a worm substitute!

What time does the balloon go up, please?

It is wonderful what a difference only a few minutes a day practice of " Harlene Hair-Drill" will achieve in the cultivation and preservation of a glorious head of hair. Friends and relations long absent will wonder at the beneficial change. Try it free for one week. Accept one of the 1,000,000 Free 4-in-1 Gift Outfits offered to readers to-day. Simply send Coupon below with your name and address and 4d. stamps for return postage and packing of parcel.

Top left: petrol became scarce, so cars were adapted to run on coal gas; women drivers were thought as comic as the weird vehicles. *Top right:* the dream postcard motif, adapted for a hair-tonic advertisement. *Below:* Poy cartoons Lloyd George's Munitions Bill, which empowered the Government to commandeer factories for adaptation to munitions work.

Opposite. Top: a German advertisement for Sanatogen. *Bottom:* small ads from the pages of *Simplicissimus* in the strange style of such advertisements in all countries, then and now.

"TURNED" TO GOOD USE.

AS IT WAS

COMMON OR GARDEN FACTORY

AS IT WILL BE.

DAVID: "Sorry to upset things, but you know what we're aiming at."

(Mr. Lloyd George's Munitions Bill empowered the Government to commandeer works which may be adapted to produce war material.)

VESTA TILLEY

Top left: the French soldier on leave comments on the new short skirt, and is told we must all make economies, my dear, it's the war. Bottom left: a hopeful British attempt to encourage economy. Top right: London theatres were packed nightly; men going home on leave especially looked forward to 'a show'. Most shows were escapist, but the male impersonator Vesta Tilley brought it all back. . . . Opposite page: in all countries the war profiteer, the man who made his pile at home, was a target for cartoonists; this one is French, but the image was universal.

The daily life of citizens in most countries was affected by food shortages. The Allied blockade of Germany resulted in rationing that soon ceased to be a joke. There was no rationing in Britain until 1918; the shortages were never so serious that they weren't good for a laugh, and the postcard industry found it a welcome new topic. The jokes were often acted out by dogs, cats or birds; a duck gazing at its lunchtime caterpillar which has escaped up a tree is captioned 'Grub's going up'. 'Substitute' ('ersatz' in the Second World War) became a joke word. Jam was said to be made of turnips, and it looked horrid in grey cardboard containers. The troops got nothing but plum-and-apple, which they groaned about endlessly. The stones from all these plums played their part; one manufacturer responded to the need to avoid waste by devising a 'Suction Gas Producer for Generating Gas from Plumstones'. The same manufacturer made another contribution to the war against waste by printing a desperate notice which said 'Use Blotting Paper to the Very Last'.

On the home front in Britain there was a boom in one tiny unimportant industry. Since the end of the nineteenth century there had been a craze for making things with the fretsaw, which could be used to cut highly intricate patterns out of thin pieces of wood. Fretwork was an effective if somewhat unprofitable way of filling up spare time; unlike the do-it-yourself movement of the present day it was dedicated not to improving the fabric of the home, but to filling it with dust-collecting knick-knacks. It had its own newspaper, *Hobbies, a Weekly Journal for Amateurs of Both Sexes*, which published designs for pipe-racks, wall mirror-brackets and, on one occasion, Milan Cathedral, with intricate detail in debased rococo, with here and there a touch of Art Nouveau. There were articles giving useful hints, and editorial comment on the state of fretwork.

Soon after war broke out the editor wrote, 'The country has now settled down to war conditions, and life is once again flowing in an almost normal manner.' Fretwork as usual. There were designs for 'The Ready-Aye-

Ready Submarine Calendar Stand', 'The Nurse Cavell Memorial Photo Frame' and 'Bomb Thrower—a particularly attractive toy at the present time'. There were models of tanks, ambulances and aircraft; 'Fall In', on the contents page, is a *Hobbies* design.

One advertisement headed 'Zeppelins be Hanged' shows Dad fretworking away in the garden, unperturbed as the raider draws near; Mum rushes out distraught, but Sonny coolly aims his fretwork aeroplane at the foe. The caption reads: 'Modern fretwork is too fascinating a pastime to be dropped for the sight of a mere Zep.' One issue of the magazine carries an article headlined 'Well-known Fretworker Killed at the Front.'

Some of the postcards, Poy's munitions cartoon and official proclamations give the impression that the civilians were having a tough time with everything geared to the war effort but other sources show that this was not so. *La Baïonnette* is full of pretty ladies in ravishing clothes, and no one in Britain seems to have been greatly influenced by the Wartime Economy Dress Exhibition. The theatres, restaurants and entertainments carried on much as usual. *Chu Chin Chow* at the Haymarket Theatre in London was a lavish oriental extravaganza with all the pop ingredients of paradise—songs and dance, slave-girls and jewels; going to see *Chu* was part of everyone's dream of Blighty.

It is easy to say that all this was an effort to put a brave face on it for the men on leave. But there were still factories making patent hair-tonics and plenty of other superfluous things—life for some went on just as before. The German advertisement for *Sanatogen* on page 127 hardly suggests overwhelming strain, and the small-ads on the same page show alongside bicycles for the war-disabled such frivolities as nose-straighteners and anti-sunburn preparation. Business as usual. Harrod's catalogue for 1917 is most revealing. A short introduction explains that 'In this third year of world-upheaval thinking men and women will . . . note with gratitude that so many of life's comforts and necessities are still obtainable and rather than deplore the imperfect fulfilment of a task beyond man's compassing they will recognize the heightened effort of this House to serve them faithfully with an unchallenged though restricted measure of resource. With great respect we dedicate this Book to that great thinking public who have made this House the House it is, and to whose continued confidence, regard and loyalty we cheerfully entrust our future.' Then, after eighty-eight pages of six-column index, it gets down to 1454 closely packed pages illustrated in the *Sanatogen* manner of popular graphics, with silver, jewelry, black cat car-mascots, purple silk-tipped cigarettes, riding habits, a 'temporary ballroom' with chandeliers, practical jokes, and the complete furnishing, food and wines of an upper middle-class household. True, there are two pages of Naval and Military Tailoring, where a few items for the Royal Flying Corps have crept in, but there are also two pages of livery for male servants. The real rationing was by price; if you had money, you could still get almost anything, just like in peacetime.

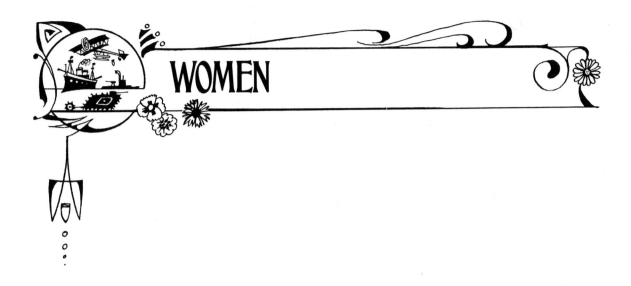

WOMEN

The most conspicuous pre-war popular images of women were:

1 The Allegorical Lady, representing Agriculture, Britannia, La Navigation, Germania, Faith, Hope or Charity. Frequently half-naked, always po-faced.

2 The Lady. Remote and delicate, with a slightly pained expression, instantly able to detect an impropriety and put it in its place.

3 The Flapper. A girl with her hair still down (i.e. teenager); pert, but certainly about to become a Lady.

4 The Flirt. A little older than the flapper, lower on the social scale, and possibly on the way to becoming

5 The Siren, or even the Woman of Easy Virtue.

6 The Deserving-poor Woman. The same pained expression as the Lady, but understandably sadder.

7 The Disreputable-poor Woman. Sometimes miserable, sometimes jolly; always a drinker.

There were also Fat Ladies, Landladies, Gorgons, and Mother-in-Law.

By the end of the war, the Lady and the Deserving-poor Woman were on their way out. The Flapper and the Flirt had become the Girl, with her variants, the Sports Girl (two-seater cars and anyone-for-tennis), the Society Girl (cigarette-holder and cocktail). The Siren prospered as the Vamp (an expression unknown before 1914). The Fat Ladies, Landladies, Gorgons and Mothers-in-Law lived on in the postcards of Donald McGill.

There was one completely new image—the Emancipated Girl, who left home and earned her own living. She featured in strip cartoons from Dot and Carrie in the *Star* to Jane of the *Daily Mirror* who kept going till well after the Second World War. She was the new-style heroine of fiction and film, with whom millions could identify and who reached her apogee in Ginger Rogers. She had emerged gradually in the quarter-century before the war but when she was noticed at all it was generally with sneers. The war was her chance for a break-through. Women, eagerly accepted where they had been barred before, did the jobs that millions of men had left, and manned the new industries.

SERBIA.   SERBIE.

Now that the age of slavery is o'er,
And the Belgian is free in the land,
Bravely with courage he reconquered
His good name, his fame and his fair flag,
And with hand now so brave and daring,
Valiant, the people will henceforth
Display upon their flag so bold and free,
For King, for Law and Liberty!

L'ANGLAISE

Les Femmes Héroïques

France.

Roumanie   Roumania

Bersagliere

Happy Japan

"A NEUTRAL"

Opposite: dozens, hundreds, of sets of postcards were produced personifying the combatants as women, who in their turn were personified as anything from amazons to butterflies. (The set of Allied butterflies had a complementary series showing the Central Powers leaders as insects, impaled on swords.)

This page: swopping hats was for many years a popular sexy gesture.

Reaction against the suffragettes in Britain before 1914 produced some really vicious graphics; the artists were, of course, men. No doubt it got them into good training for the beastly anti-enemy graphics that became so popular as soon as the war started. By 1918 the images of the women working in the factories and on the land, in hospitals and in the forces, unlike those of the soldiers at the front, were still heroic and dashing. Even the comic ones were pretty.

The troops understandably wanted pin-ups for the dug-out. Paintings by artists like Kirchner were reproduced by the thousand, winsome, ladylike, cheeky or sexy dream-girls.

The Allegorical Ladies were a late-baroque hang-over. They were familiar to all, their light draperies were faintly daring and, being standardized, they gave the artist little trouble. Though few of the posters on which they appear carry dates, and postcards, which might have legible datemarks, rarely featured these ladies, it is safe to assume that they all belong to the early years of the war. 'The Awakening of Wales' on page 139 was certainly published in 1915, an amazing frontispiece to *The Land of My Fathers* (proceeds of sales to Welsh troops). What can they have made of this in the land of Chapel and Sunday closing?

There were a lot of other unlikely ladies. The artist simply painted a pretty girl in his own personal style and then clapped a military hat on, or draped a flag around her; different pose for each ally, add name of country and he had a new set of postcards—there were dozens and dozens of such sets. Some of them came in full military uniform, with swords, or cycling off to the front with no weapons at all. Some were unmilitary but noble, wearing national costume, some were Surrealist with butterfly wings.

Sergt-Major Flora Sandes was an unlikely lady without any help from the postcard artist (page 137). The caption on the back tells us that 'this plucky Irish lady' was 'for two years fighting with the Serbian army which she joined as a private. Sergt-Major Sandes has taken part in all fighting, and was badly wounded at the taking of Hill 1212. She has been awarded the highest decoration for which Serbian Soldiers are eligible. Early this year, while home on leave, [she] assisted in collecting for the Hon. Mrs Haverfield's Society for Providing Comforts for the Serbian Soldiers and Prisoners of War [and] had the honour of being received by Queen Alexandra at Marlborough House.'

There was plenty of action at home too; at one British factory when the munitions had been made for the day, female employees could work off surplus energy in their own football team, 'The Munitionettes'.

A lot of women did no war-work and so never got into clothes as universally awful as the things worn by munition workers and land girls. It has been said that all the various shapeless sacks were specially designed to keep sex at bay. At least the overalls and uniforms, however hideous, were much more comfortable to live in than the pre-war fashions: steel-boned corsets, wired neck-lines and hobble-skirts were happily discarded and have never come back.

In four years inches came off the length of the skirt and went on to its width, so that it was possible to jump on a bus. Make-up, which had been a sure sign of sin for more than a century, went back on the face, and even Ladies smoked (cigarettes only, and never in the street).

The Ladies, in fact, took full advantage of the freedoms won by the Women who Worked, and gradually they lost their identity (Daphne, whose dainty silk-clad ankles tripped graciously through the books of Dornford Yates between the wars, was the last real Lady.)

Left: a patriotic all-American mum. *Right top and middle:* two views of a box to lend an extra something to a wartime engagement ring. The ring shown in it is made of clear glass, white and scarlet beads, and was sold in Britain for Red Cross charities. *Bottom:* a leather purse in the shape of a German service cap.

Je t'aime! m'aimes-tu?

DIX
810/5

Je t'aime! m'aimes-tu?
C'est l'heure des vendanges...
Au diable la Vertu,
Viens! allons voir les anges!

WORKING IN 'SHIFTS'
AND NO 'BLOOMERS'!!

FRED SPURGIN

NATIONAL SERVICE

Sunshine on the Land

DRIVEN FROM HOME BY A WOMAN

FRED SPURGIN

◄ *Top row:* love was a constant theme on postcards, here in French, American and British form. French kisses look best. *Bottom row:* three British cards, soft and comic, showing women doing war work.

SERGEANT-MAJOR FLORA SANDES
THE ONLY BRITISH WOMAN IN THE SERBIAN ARMY

Top left: a munition worker, an image which gets a bit nearer the real thing, though she is handling the case of explosives as if presenting a dish of grapes in a musical comedy; the odalisque image dies hard. *Top right:* a Crest china munition worker, with the arms of Glasgow across her stomach, surrounded by her produce. *Bottom right:* there are always a few women who want to fight and do.

Not many Ladies can have carried on like the one in the following poem. It was printed on a postcard, surrounded by red crosses, maps of the continents and angels blowing trumpets. On the back of one copy, the sender wrote, 'this is what a Friend of Mrs Rossington wrote his selfe I thought it would be nice for you to read.'

Angels have no Nationality
A True Story of the Great European War

She was wife of an English officer of noble name,
Full dressed as a Flemish peasant woman, with certain aim,
Sufficiently disguised throughout—indeed a perfect ruse—
Head-dress, with spectacles, ear-rings, basket and native shoes.

Ah! Yes, that wonderful disguise was good enough for sure,
It took her where she wished to be, amid the cannons' roar;
It let her see for once, sights she would never see again,
It made her feel as ne'er before for thousands now in pain.

Passing along, a wounded German she observed to stand,
And try to bandage up afresh, a shattered arm and hand,
She went at once, and did the work so gently and so well,
That he begged her to accept from him a five franc bill.

But just as gently she refused, and then he asked her why,
'Why could not he her valued services reward— not buy?'

'Because I am an English woman, Sir, if you would know;'
'Excuse Madame—Do you expect me to believe that true?

'English or no—Surely you are an angel—that I see,
'And angels my dear Madame, have no nationality;
'But silently you go to work, with loving heart and hand;
'You recognize no man as foe, no place as alien land.'

'But may I kiss your hand' said he, as tears then filled his eyes,
Wishing to show his gratitude, to lady in disguise;
And for reply, she gave her hand this German for to kiss,
To kiss an angel by the way would not be far amiss.

Angels there are in every land, who move with gentle tread
To bind and heal, to soothe, and kneel beside the sufferer's bed,
Thrice welcome for the work they do, believing they are given,
To help to make life bearable, and give us glimpse of heaven.

(From *Life and Poems of John D. Fox*)

Opposite. Top left: The Awakening of Wales; bare breasts have always been acceptable for allegories, even in the most puritanical quarters. *Top right:* a popular tear-jerker. *Middle right:* more sweat-less munitions work. *Bottom:* a stolid America, printed in Italy; an Italian dream of the warrior's return; and an English postcard interpreting the nation's most popular war song.

Her Cross.

FOOD FOR THE GUNS.

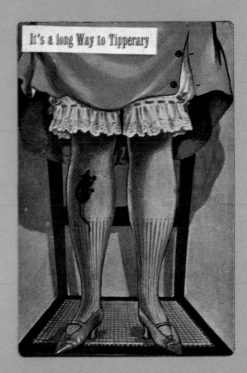

It's a long Way to Tipperary

CHILDREN

'Bang, bang! You're dead!' Ever since there were guns, small boys have played at war with this cry as the final solution, a formula that has the advantage of leaving the enemy alive to go on with the game.

Pre-war nursery battles had been fought with toy firearms, swords and horses made of wood, varied by the centuries-old survival of toy bows and arrows, useful for an occasional game of Robin Hood. Folded paper hats were worn; all the equipment was very simple, even when cowboys became fashionable. Imaginary war enjoyed the airy freedom of imaginary equipment.

One of the most ancient human desires is to own miniature men, whether for magic, or just for playing games. During the Renaissance superb model soldiers were made in silver and gold as collectors' pieces. Fine models are made to this day, but these are grown-ups' playthings. Probably the first that could really be called toys were made in the eighteenth century in Nuremberg. By the middle of the nineteenth century demand was widespread and Germany had a near monopoly of the whole industry. The figures were cast or stamped out flat in alloys of lead and tin. The later, hollow, men were a British invention which by 1914 had been adopted by most makers. A box of toy soldiers was in every boy's Christmas stocking—attempts to turn belligerent children from war were put in their place by Saki in his nasty tale *Toys of Peace*. By 1914 the manufacturers were also persuading children that they needed proper boxed toy uniforms, and the paper cocked hat died.

Above: babies in uniform; a chocolate soldier mould. *Opposite:* obverse and reverse of a linen print for making up into a soldier doll; recently re-issued by the Victoria and Albert Museum, London.

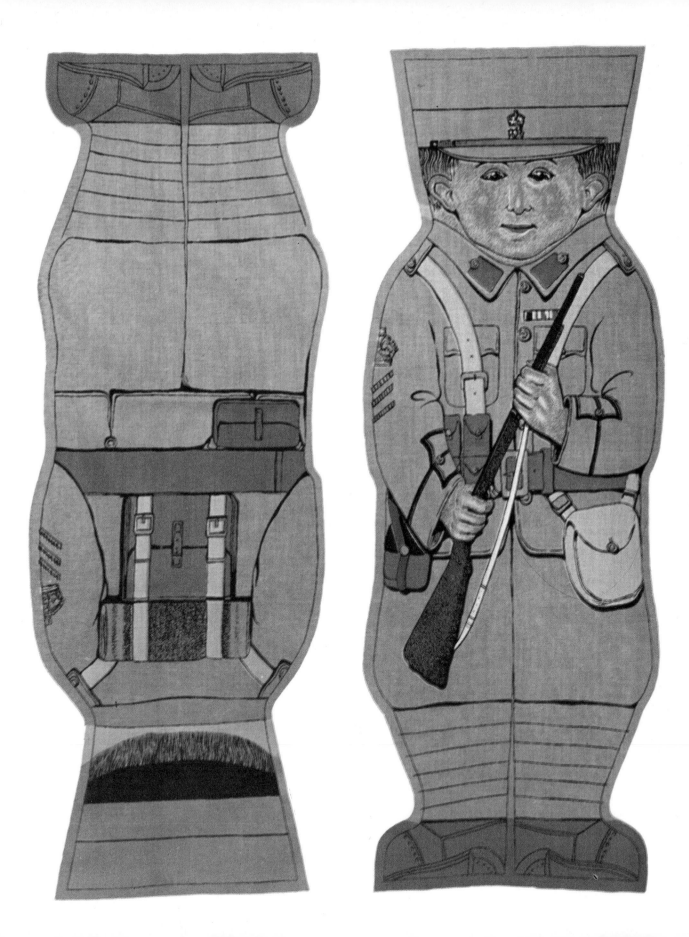

Whatever people feel about nursery battle-
fields, many will find distasteful the way
children were used in the Great War to por-
tray adult fantasies. On postcards especially,
every aspect of the war was re-enacted with
babies or small children as the participants.
Allied babies waved flags, national stereotypes
became uniformed toddlers paralleling the
grown-up versions—all quite harmless and
often very charming.

However, children were soon made use of
in the postcard hate-campaigns, and sinister
little scenes appear showing tiny allies ganging
up on another tot forced to impersonate the
enemy. Children played all parts—gallant
lads, cynical Old Bills, food hoarders, jolly
sailors, casualties with attendant tiny nurses;
there are even heartless jokes about shirkers
and conscientious objectors.

PETITS ALLIÉS
LITTLE BOYS ALLIED

PATRIOTIC
1056

Un bagno inaspettato   Un bain inattendu

Opposite. Right: 'Just Like Daddy', a plaster statuette, a horrid but hypnotic little
creature. *Left:* just like Mummy and Daddy, outfits for a fancy dress party. *This
page. Top left:* Allied babies on a French card. *Top right:* this German card is
captioned 'Interrogating a prisoner'. The sender wrote on the back, 'This represents
the great astonishment amongst the Germans on a captured Scotch prisoner being
brought before them. They don't know whether it is a boy or girl.' *Middle left:* an
Italian card, 'An unexpected bathe', shows the flooding of the Belgian dykes. *Middle
right:* an Austrian soldier goes off to war. *Below left:* Donald McGill makes light
of the internment camp. *Below right:* an American 'Smile Messenger' card puns on
the Hospital Blue of the wounded.

INTERNED !

*No Blues
When there's news
Of You's*

India, All Hail!

"Sons of the Empire" ④ — Copyright

Eyes right!

THE WAR BABY
(Undress Uniform)

LES CHANSONS DE FRANCE
de MAURICE BOUKAY

LES ORPHELINS DE LA GUERRE

GET OUT OF YOUR CIVILIAN CLOTHES AND GET INTO KHAKI

Dere go my Civies!

SOUTH AFRICA
South Africa beyond the Sea,—
Oh, thats the Sunny home for me!
But I have heard the British Drum
Beating to Arms!— and here I come!

DENKT AN UNSERE KRIEGER-WAISEN!

Kameraden Vorsicht bei Gesprächen

L'assaut.
Cheer up.
Ataka.

You always were a LITTLE CLIPPER!

PORTUGAL

"Alpha"

A Conscientious Objector

Opposite: (1) A German card of at least ten years before the war with baby soldiers already at military exercise. (2) 'India, All Hail' is from one of the many Sons of Empire series. (3) The French child pissing into a German helmet is called Seed of the Soldier, i.e. a chip off the old block. (4) Mabel Lucie Atwell's beloved Pooksie appears as a staff officer, smoking on duty. (5) A very serious French Red Cross card. (6) Negro jokes were not yet in bad taste. (7) Another Son of Empire. (8) German child ('Think of the War Orphans!') seems to be raising funds by pointing out that his stein is empty. (9) Precocious French infants. *L'assaut* was translated into 'Cheer Up' for the English market. (10) Women filled jobs on the railways—another role to be enacted by the juveniles. (11) Portuguese children from an 'Allies' series. (12) An odd twist to the 'conchie' theme.

This page. Top: a little wooden Hun, a product of the German cottage toy industry. *Middle:* a warship made of wooden building blocks; an utterly restrictive and uncreative toy, as this is the only meaningful arrangement. However, one hit from a well-aimed nursery cannon, and the whole thing would go up just like Beatty's did at Jutland. *Bottom:* post-war German toy tanks made in tin-plate and driven by clockwork—all of them on wheels, except for one in the front which has rubber tracks. The left-hand one is not far from the Mark VIII Anglo-American 'International' model (which never saw war service); the rest are based on the Mark V somewhat embellished.

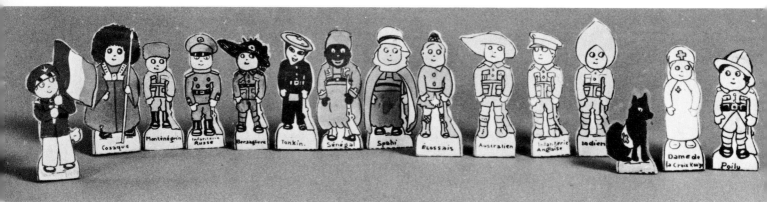

Cosaque · Monténégrin · Infanterie Russe · Bersaglière · Tonkin. · Sénégal · Spahi · Ecossais · Australien · Infanterie Anglaise · Indien · Dame de la Croix Rouge · Poilu

Top left: get the red, white and blue balls into the Kaiser's mouth; on the back 'Bitter Pills for Kaiser Bill'. *Top right:* small toys, hand-made and manufactured. The Bleriot aircraft was a pre-war French toy to which roundels were added. The wooden ones are German. *Middle:* cut-out Allies, of all colours, made in France. *Bottom right:* a French machine-gunner.

(1) Interwar British small-scale lead soldiers (Dinky Toy and Skybirds).
(2) British machine gunners, dispatch rider and a watcher of the skies.
(3) German flat soldiers; infantry firing at advancing Russians. (4)
German flat models; cavalry. (5) German flat models; machines of war.
(6) French sentry. (7) Swedish pewter flat soldiers of the Finnish Army.
(8) Swedish pewter flat models, Mannerheim on horseback and in his staff
car; and a Renault tank with Finnish swastika, an Allied vehicle with which
to attack ex-ally Russia (9) Injection-moulded German soldiers of 1914
vintage (Airfix, late 1960s).

The manufacturers of toy wars were as stimulated by the real war as the other manufacturers; they too had a great new range of subjects. Those on the Allied side got an even greater bonus—the German toy industry, the biggest, best, and cheapest in Europe, was cut off from its markets. In Britain toys were aggressively labelled *British Made*. The Lord Robert's Memorial Workshops, which employed wounded soldiers, made wooden lorries and ships which carried little brass plates whose inscriptions make it clear that the toys were not imported contraband.

Most of the war toys were for boys. Little girls were not held to be addicted to bang-bangery, and the things marketed for them during the war did not differ very much from those of peacetime. There were soldier and sailor dolls, Red Cross nurse dolls with hospital-blue dolls to look after, and junior knitting kits that enabled little girls to sit making socks for soldiers, but that was about their lot. They simply had to keep the home fires burning in the dolls' houses, and were generally condemned to the role of patient Penelopes. Quite unlike many of their mothers, who, as we have seen, were by now having a much more interesting time.

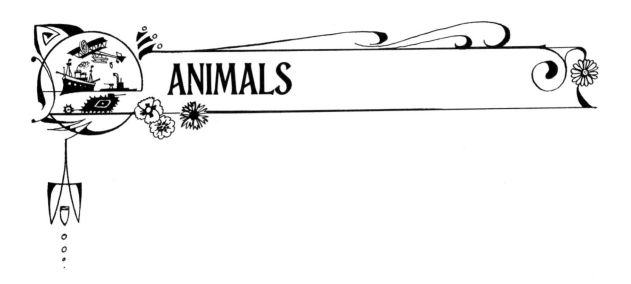

ANIMALS

Certain animals played important roles in the Great War, both practical and symbolic, and held a significant place in the popular arts.

Horses were used for transport everywhere throughout the war, and cavalry, though condemned to a war of frustration on the Western Front, was active in less constricted campaigns. The horse retained its symbolic role as the mount of the war leader, and at a more humble level as man's faithful friend. Horses had flag-days (*Their Day*, page 120), their own hospitals run by the Blue Cross, and were portrayed in many paintings and toys. There was even a tiny tin horse-ambulance with an equine casualty inside and another horse to pull him to safety.

Dogs were trained to work at the front, carrying messages and sniffing out snipers. They were depicted sentimentally as man's other faithful friend, waiting at home; they also assumed a role denied to the horse, as national symbols—bull-dog for Britain, poodle for France, borzoi for Russia. The Central Powers, though in general sticking to their eagles, used the wolf-hound for themselves, and showed bull-dogs and poodles as nasty, cowardly, snarling creatures. The Allies promptly retaliated with the sausage dog (dachshunds were said to have been stoned in London in 1914 for being German).

In sickness or in health, dog and horse tie for first place as Man's Noblest Friend.

PALS!

The Triple Entente

"Destroyer and Submarine"

Top: noble Allied dogs from Russia, Britain and France, and one of F. E. Morgan's endearing pussies.
Middle: four British cards. *Bottom:* a German Easter card, with Central Powers Easter Eggs; the Japanese
representative from a series of patriotic Allied chicks; two more British cards.

To Arms

At last!

WE SHELL!

A MASCOT

Oh, no! I'm not back from the Front!
I've just had a <u>chat</u> with a friend of mine!

Pacifist, or Conscientious Objector

Le Japonais   The Japanese

"I'VE GOT MY
WORM TICKET."

I'VE GOT A BLIGHTY.

Right: the head of 'Tirpitz', the famous pig rescued after the sinking of the German cruiser *Dresden,* and a Breeches Buoy from the same ship (not, alas, used to rescue the pig, who was picked up gallantly swimming). *Below:* this engaging creature was made by a member of the Chinese Labour Force in France.

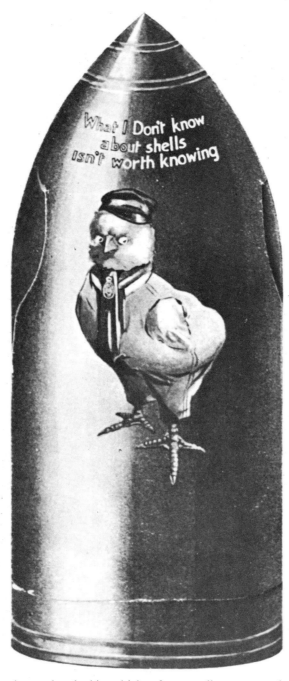

A truculent looking chicken from a pull-out postcard of views of Bristol.
Opposite: a powerful Kaiser Cat by Louis Wain, which pre-figures his later patterned and finally schizophrenic cats.

Cats were carried on warships to fight the mice, and some became hero-cats, like Jimmy of HMS *Renown*, but most of them sensibly stayed at home, trading on their reputation for being hard to train. Cats were used for rationing jokes and other comic situations, and as good luck symbols. Pre-war pretty-pussy cards were given a new lease of life with topical wartime captions.

Pigeons were used throughout the war to carry messages, as they had since Napoleonic times. British pigeoneers were part of the Royal Engineers, and kept their pigeons in converted London buses (see page 68). Hero pigeons were given medals, and when they went to their happy homing grounds they were stuffed and kept in regimental museums.

The Royal Navy actually attempted to train sea-lions and even seagulls to spot enemy submarines. Following dummy periscopes was rewarded with a hand out of fish, but the trainees proved incapable of making the transference necessary to seek out the periscopes of the enemy. The navy kept very quiet about this escapade, so unfortunately it never came to the attention of the professional humorists.

The cockerel stood for France, crowing triumphantly in a cap of liberty. Domestic cocks and hens acted out sex-war jokes on postcards just as they had for the previous decade, with added wartime twists like the puns about shells. All very predictable; less so was the postcard series in which belligerent chicks emerged from eggs, wearing military headgear and waving national flags.

The bear stood for Russia, strong, indomitable but cuddly in Allied cartoons; bumbling, overweight and crafty in German ones.

The human attitude to pigs has been ambivalent for centuries. Symbols of greed, dirt and beastliness, they have also been singled out for intelligence and luck, trained as truffle hunters and as learned pigs in circuses. As the Germans were known to eat a lot of pork, and used pigs on New Year greetings cards, their symbolic wartime role was clear to the Allies. The Germans seem to have continued to see pigs as pigs.

No country took the mule to its heart,

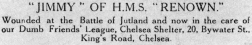

"JIMMY" OF H.M.S. "RENOWN."
Wounded at the Battle of Jutland and now in the care of
our Dumb Friends' League, Chelsea Shelter, 20, Bywater St.,
King's Road, Chelsea.

Left: a very gallant pussy. *Above:* carving by Phyllis Bone from the Scottish National War Memorial, Edinburgh, showing canaries and mice. Tunnellers used them (like miners did) to detect bad air or gas, because they die sooner than humans.

though it was the most hard worked of all animals, carrying packs and dragging guns through appalling conditions in all climates. It was, of course, proverbially stubborn, though the Oxford English Dictionary says that this reputation is 'without good grounds'; it was also famous for its kick—this certainly was true. It remained unloved and unexploited as a symbol. Another animal mystery was the general failure of either side to see the enemy as an ass.

An unforgivable lack of imagination on the part of the British authorities denied the mole a deserved place in the ranks of the symbolic animals. When a special unit of miners and sewer workers was formed to tunnel under the enemy to blow him up, or to tunnel under his tunnellers and blow *them* up, some right-minded officer suggested that they should be called the Moles; his reasonable suggestion went unheeded. To think that they might have had as their motto that terrible cry, the climax of *The Wind in the Willows*, 'A Mole! A Mole!'

PEACE & COMMEMORATION

Peace, agreed six hours before in a railway carriage at Compiègne, came at the eleventh hour on the eleventh day of the eleventh month, 1918—the magic touch of symbolism was powerful to the last. The Americans kept the gun that fired the last shell of the war, and so did everyone else.

To the survivors it was quite unreal; it was over, it wasn't going on any more, you could stand up in no-man's-land. Peace came dropping slow, though John Brophy tells how 'at a hospital, not far from Etaples, a Scottish RAMC officer recklessly signed an order—which was duly posted in the wards—declaring: "To celebrate the conclusion of hostilities, every patient will be allowed an extra piece of bread and jam with his tea".'

Allied civilians rushed straight into the wildest celebrations, especially in London, where the cheering, singing, dancing, bonfires, drinking and sex went on for days and nights on end, to the music of that beloved British tune, breaking glass. Flags and impromptu street decorations went up, and later there were parades and processions. In the Paris streets piles of surrendered German guns were tipped nosedown to symbolize defeat. Some guns were brought to Britain, and ended up as trophies behind railings in provincial towns.

The home-based fire-eaters regretted that the Allies had not marched on Berlin and razed it to the ground, and no efforts could put the build-up of propaganda into reverse smartly enough to still the almost universal cries of 'Hang the Kaiser!'

When the bombing and gunfire ceased life in Britain must have seemed rather quiet, but after the signing of the Peace Treaty at Versailles, the bangs came back again in the most splendid of all the popular arts, fireworks, with the biggest display ever staged. It was held in Hyde Park and it included portraits of the King and Queen, heroes and patriotic slogans, a final flight of two thousand rockets and a cascade a thousand feet long.

At the Crystal Palace there were regular firework displays which included pictorial set-pieces of the Battle of Jutland, the attack on Zeebrugge and a Zeppelin raid on London.

The Palace itself reopened with The Great Victory Exhibition, shown on the next page. It was a splendid hodge-podge of everything that had been saved, with no nonsense about glass cases. It stayed there for several years, with the dummy parachutist and the sniper's tree getting dustier and more ghastly. Pruned of its tatters, it is now housed in the Imperial War Museum in London. Most of the winning countries have similar museums, and there are also local and private collections.

Top: a pile of captured German guns, aeroplanes and other detritus of war piled up in a Paris street and crowned by a triumphant French cockerel. *Bottom:* in June 1920 the Crystal Palace on the outskirts of London (which had been used as a naval depot during the war) was re-opened by the King and Queen as the Imperial War Museum and Great Victory Exhibition, all set up within the framework of the nineteenth-century Palace displays. Here 'Latest Types of British Aircraft' amongst the Kings and Queens of England.

CRYSTAL PALACE. IMPERIAL WAR MUSEUM
AND GREAT VICTORY EXHIBITION.

LATEST TYPES OF BRITISH AIRCRAFT

Fashions in war memorials and military cemeteries have changed over the centuries. The accent used to be on the glorification of victory; memorials to the fallen are comparatively recent. Though some permanent monuments were built while the war was still going on, the real commemoration explosion came after it was all over. While the fighting was still on, bodies were buried more or less where they fell; the graves were marked with wooden crosses, with name, rank and unit painted on (troops often passed truckloads of blank crosses and even empty coffins on their way up to the front). Different nations had different shaped crosses, and there was provision for non-Christians—Moslems had a vertical plank with the top profiled like a little turban. Temporary graves were sometimes done up in popular taste, like the one on page 118; a helmet or a broken rifle added a personal touch. An airman often had his propeller planted over him.

The war dead presented a massive tidying-up operation. North-eastern France was covered with cemeteries—French, Belgian, British, German, mixed—some huge, some with only two or three graves. Many men had no known grave, many bodies no name. Britain handed over the designing of its cemeteries in France and Belgium to the architectural establishment—Lutyens, Baker and Blomfield, the pomp and circumstance brigade of Edwardian Imperialism. Their task was to design permanent cemeteries where a final home could be found for every body (no one was prepared to face transporting them all home as the Americans do now), and where the names of the missing could be recorded.

The architects must have had a fairly free hand over cost, and they reacted with a considerable avoirdupois of building. The cemeteries vary in size and in the larger ones great ingenuity was used to diminish the appalling repetition, a euphemistic softening of the enormous truth. Walls, hedges and changes in level break up the lines of crosses; each grave has its own little group of flowers, different from the one next door—the ultimate triumph of the suburban ethos (Lutyens in his early years had a lot to do with establishing the Surrey style). It is all as neat as Surbiton, beautifully kept to this day.

France, perhaps numbed by her losses, reacted with the deepest aesthetic insensibility. Admittedly it was a bad period for French architecture, but the vast monument at Verdun is bad even for its date. Round it stretch row after row of crosses—no sign here of any attempt to soften the blow.

The Germans had a difficult problem with their cemeteries in France and Belgium. They had been the invaders, they had lost. They had nothing to celebrate and no one was going to give them more land than was necessary. Whether it was for this reason, or out of an atavistic attitude, many of their cemeteries are mass graves. Some would hold that this did less than justice to the men who died (but in the Great War life was not prized very highly), and some would hold that the British accent on the individual was hypocrisy born of guilt. Either way, the German architects made these melancholy places into works of art, little known and underrated. The cemetery at Langemarck, near Ypres, is simply a large square grove of regularly planted oak trees, growing straight out of the grass, with here and there groups of low stone crosses like clumps of mushrooms in the shade. Round it all is a broad low drystone wall capped with turf, and in one corner is a ruined German pill-box surrounded by yellow flowers. At the gates is a book with the thousands of names of the dead. No pomp, no piles of masonry, but poetry that catches at the throat.

Top: 'Tranchée des Baïonnettes' at Verdun. *Bottom:* German trench rebuilt as a monument, the sandbags being filled with concrete. Now the sacking has rotted away leaving only its imprint on the cement. *Opposite:* British front line at Hill 62 near Ypres.

GERMAN FRONT
APRIL 9 1917

The Canadians' Newfoundland Park, near Vimy, also succeeds in touching the emotions where so many of the architectural pomposities fail. There is a wood of Canadian trees; through the wood is the front line and, beyond a tiny strip of grass that was once no-man's-land, is the German line.

A French attempt to make a memorial of the actual field of battle is crushed with monumentality. The Tranchée des Baïonnettes at Verdun commemorates an incident during a bombardment when a trench caved in and a group of men were buried where they stood. Only their bayonets remained visible, sticking through the mud. The story became a legend, and a ponderous concrete bunker was built over the spot, which became a national shrine. But there is no poetry here.

Here and there, local people commemorated the war by preserving bits of trench and making them into tourist attractions. Some are probably sham; all are 'improved'. There is a very good one behind a café at Hill 62 near Ypres. In the café are slot-machines where you can spend hours looking at grisly 3-D photographs of the war. Behind the café a path leads down through a wood, with shell cases and rusting guns in the ferns on either side, to the trench—its sides shored up with corrugated iron, with here and there a rifle propped against it. At the bottom, duckboards swim in water, just like then; on the parapet, a tin hat with a hole in it and a flower growing through. Among the younger trees, the occasional shattered trunk, petrified by shell fire. A surrealist and evocative landscape.

Several nations claim the invention of the Tomb of the Unknown Warrior (Walt Whitman had had the idea during the American Civil War); each had its own technique for choosing its soldier. The British had six unrecognizable (but British) corpses dug up from six battle areas by an impartial commission and put in identical coffins. 'The unknown remains were placed in a hut, each draped with the Union Jack. All concerned then retired to a distance. Lastly "a British officer of very high rank" was blindfolded, and led into the hut, which he had not previously entered. Groping about, he finally touched one of the coffins and so selected the Unknown Warrior.' (J. Brophy and E. Partridge *The Long Trail*). The corpse was put in a coffin of British oak with a tattered Union Jack from Hill 60 as a shroud, and buried in Westminster Abbey in soil from Ypres. All over the Empire, bereaved fiancées were convinced it was *their* boy. The French buried their *Soldat Inconnu* under the Arc de Triomphe, where an eternal flame burns.

London Road, Royal Tunbridge Wells.

Northern France before the war was covered with cornfields, full of the flowers that grew among crops before the era of weedkillers. The poppy was the most conspicuous of them, almost the colour of fresh blood, opening thin creased petals in the morning, dead by evening; the war poets made everyone see it vividly. After the war, poppies became a symbol of remembrance, and were sold in Britain for the Haig Memorial Fund on 11 November. Since the fund also helps the victims of later wars, Poppy Day remains Britain's biggest flag-day. The flowers are made by the disabled; some large early silk ones for twisting round the mascots of rich cars were exquisitely done, but modern ones are plastic and they don't look much like poppies any more.

Opposite: Postcards cheerfully celebrated peace. Haig poppies commemorate the dead. The British Mons Star, General Service Medal and Victory Medal, called Pip, Squeak and Wilfred, after the *Daily Mirror* strip cartoon characters, were worn by civilians on 11th November, and by those who failed to make it back in Civvy Street, when selling matches in the gutter. *This page. Top:* many towns and villages got a tank to keep as a memento, and they sat rusting away on prominent sites for years; most of them were melted down for armaments during the Second World War. *Right:* the Tomb of the Unknown Soldier in Paris, where a Flame of Remembrance burns under the Arc de Triomphe, built in 1806, when allies were enemies.

ICI REPOSE UN SOLDAT FRANÇAIS MORT POUR LA PATRIE 1914 1918

PARIS. - La Tombe du Soldat Inconnu sous l'Arc de Triomphe
The Tomb of the unknown Soldier under Triumph Arch

M

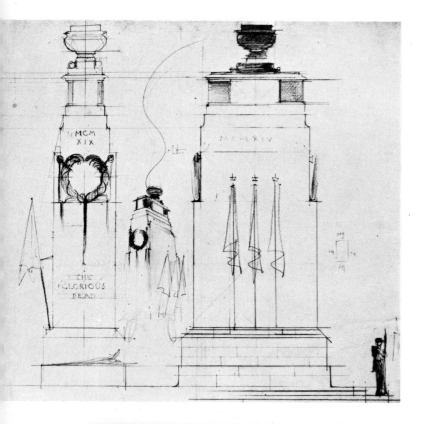

Near Westminster Abbey, in Whitehall, a cenotaph was built to an uncharacteristically modest design by Lutyens. On 11 November every year, the reigning monarch placed a wreath there, maroons sounded and there was a two minute silence in memory of the dead. All work, all traffic stopped, and thousands stood with bowed heads; the silence was only broken by the wing-beats of pigeons startled by the bangs and the bugles.

The cenotaph held its mystique for many years, and men sitting on buses raised their hats to it. Armistice Day has now been moved from 11 November to the nearest Sunday—the weekday disruption is no longer acceptable. The young can't remember what the bangs are for but the pigeons still whirl.

Every town and parish had its memorial, and so did many schools and factories; they were popular subjects for postcards—one showed the memorial to the fallen of the local gas works.

The Crest industry found the cenotaph a most appropriate mantelshelf object and turned out thousands in many sizes and varieties of shape. They also made models of town memorials, and fireplaces inscribed 'We've kept the Home Fires Burning'. Some models of British memorials are marked 'Foreign' and some 'Saxony'; Germany was getting back into the markets. Handymen made their own memorials and *Hobbies* published a design for a 'Fretwork Home Cenotaph'.

The Times IN MEMORIAM column still reminds British readers every day of the young men who died more than fifty years ago. The names of the war dead head the column, separated from the civilians by a neat line. 'In proud and loving memory . . .', 'On this his birthday . . .', 'At Loos', 'On 1 July 1916'. Occasionally a shrill note of resentment cracks the rhythm—'Murdered at Vimy . . .'.

Opposite. Top: Sir Edwin Lutyens's sketch for the Cenotaph in London. The urn (for an eternal flame) was abandoned.
Bottom: a cardboard model money-box of the Cenotaph.
This page. Top: the Cenotaph became a popular image overnight, and the Crest manufacturers turned them out in all sizes (and many shapes) for the mantelshelf. They also made models of town war memorials.
Bottom: amateurs found the Cenotaph an apt subject, though they didn't bother too much about Lutyens's classical proportions; one author thoughtfully added a clock, something Lutyens forgot.

One of the many private memorial cards; a photograph encircled by laurels like the ones placed live on countless graves and war memorials.

Above: a remarkable German postcard printed for the Allied market. It shows the heads of state of Belgium, France, Britain, Italy and, lower, USA with assorted Valkyries and Britannia carrying scales of justice. A view of Cologne Cathedral fills the space below. The sender wrote on the back, 'What do you think of the Germans printing a thing like this. It's like their honour, as thick as their skin.' This rather grovelling attempt to get back into the export business was bound to come up against sales resistance.

Opposite: a cast-iron German frame; oak leaves for a dead hero.

164

Top: thousands of souvenirs were manufactured from waste metal, both during and after the war. The *pickel-haube* on a stand made from bullets is for decoration only, but the Souvenir de Verdun (left) is an inkwell. The large double inkwell in the form of a gun turret is CAST FROM METAL EX-SURRENDERED GERMAN BATTLESHIP HELGOLAND. Alas, the guns are not pens. *Bottom:* the Great War is still recalled in objects made today like the Japanese wooden puzzle tank and the collectors' model soldiers; the lead cavalrymen, with horses in eighteenth-century attitudes, were bought in Denmark in 1967. The two aircraft at the back were made by Bill Howell with felt-nib pen fuselages and fishermen's line-winders for wings; next to them is one made from a dart with pigeon's feather wings. The small aeroplanes are modern Hong Kong plastic toys.

Souvenirs, made or picked up on the battle-fields, were carefully kept, and Dad's medals were put in a frame and hung beside the photographs of heroic uncles.

Tank paperweights and machine gun ink-wells were sold as souvenirs at Vimy and Verdun, and in Belgium a flourishing cottage-industry made ashtrays and crucifixes out of bullets, buttons and badges, to sell to tourists and Old-Comrades Associations revisiting the familiar places. French farmers round the Somme made practical use of the *objets trouvés* in their fields, and to this day many of their fences are made of Great War barbed wire.

The Second World War produced little popular art. The cultural climate had altered, houses were no longer so cluttered with little objects and the creative impulses found other outlets. Industry was controlled so that frivolities were no longer permitted, and the control of paper allowed less printed ephemera. Men in workshops still made brass objects in their spare time, but these were mostly cigarette-lighters or ash-trays. Brass aeroplanes were made, but the less intricate streamlined shapes of aircraft were best reproduced by solid castings, and they are not at all imaginative. Italian prisoners left behind in Britain some model tanks and aeroplanes which are in the spirit of the Great War ones, but they stand alone. Combat aircraft themselves still carried painted mascots; here it was the Americans who excelled, using sexy film stars and Walt Disney animals. But there wasn't much else.

Throughout the four years of the First World War, in all the countries involved, amateurs working away in their spare time and professionals designing for popular tastes between them created a fantasy counterpart to reality which contains its own truths. If we set what they made beside the songs which Joan Littlewood collected in *Oh, What A Lovely War!* and the slang and recitations that Eric Partridge and John Brophy recorded in *The Long Trail*, we begin to understand more of the Great War than if we only read the histories, visit museums, or look at photographs and official paintings.

What we have shown and described in this book are fragments of the greatest explosion of wartime popular art there has ever been.

Nothing quite like it will ever happen again.

VON DER WELT VERLASSEN

The Kaiser in exile
'By the World For-
gotten', and one of
Bairnsfather's last
Old Bills.

"'Ullo!"

[*November 11, 1918*]

Photograph and drawings acknowledgement

The photograph of the Russian Easter egg was taken by Derrick Witty. All the other objects were photographed by Bill Howell.

The line drawings on pages 10, 44, 45, 56–60, 75, 76, 98, 108, 117, 120, 156, 157 and 164 are by Barbara Jones.

Acknowledgements

We would like to offer our thanks to the following: the staff of the Imperial War Museum, London, for much invaluable help; Miss Mary Adshead for lending us a Princess Mary gift box designed by her father; John and Venetia Newall for allowing the Russian Easter egg from their collection to be photographed; the Royal Institute of British Architects Drawings Collection for permission to reproduce Lutyens' Cenotaph drawing; the Victoria and Albert Museum for permission to reproduce the cut-out soldier doll; the Norfolk County Library for the Hobbies material; the Earl Haig Poppy Factory for the wreath of poppies; Private J. C. Whitmill, ex-Royal Marines, for the loan of his medals, and the Vicar of St Stephen's, Hampstead, for lending us the Union Jack in the frontispiece. Finally, we must thank our friends among the antique and junk dealers, through whose hands most of these objects have passed into ours; what men with spades are to archaeologists, they have been to us; without them, we would have found little.

Notes to the illustrations

The following notes give in millimetres the largest dimensions of the objects shown in the illustrations; exceptions are indicated. Nationality is given where known.

Unless otherwise stated, all objects are from the Bill Howell collection, and all postcards from the authors' collections. I.W.M. stands for 'By courtesy of the Trustees of the Imperial War Museum', Lambeth Road, London S.W.1.

Frontispiece Metal place, 255 mm. British. 1919.
    King Albert bust, 172 mm. 'Wy Knot' Crest China. British.
    Red Cross, 80 mm. French.
    Jack-in-the-box shell, 165 mm fully extended. German.
    Wooden shell, 160 mm. Belgian, 1915.
    Brass mug, 130 mm. British.
    Wool embroidery, 705 mm. British.

Page 5 Fretwork pattern. *Hobbies* January-July 1915 p.316. Norfolk County Library. British.

6 Kitchener mug, 160 mm. British.
    Old Bill mug, 112 mm. British.

8 Shrapnel dagger, 162 mm. British.

9 Brass biplane, 57 mm wingspan.
    Service cap, 85 mm.

    Tank, 130 mm over base.
    Submarine, 163 mm.
    Zeppelin, 52 mm.
    Spoons, 213 mm.

10 Aeroplanes, left to right, 35, 35 and 45 mm.
    Cup and saucer, 116 mm. 'K.P.M.' German.
    Powder box, 94 mm. French.

11 F. Fleming *Troupes Ecossaises Revenant du Combat* Musée du Luxembourg, Paris.

12 Royal Naval Air Service armoured car, 120 mm. British.

13 Poster. I.W.M. Brazilian.

15 *Simplicissimus* April-September 1916, p. 117. German.

16 'The Proudest Moment of His Life', 120 mm. Presumed Australian.

17 Wooden bust, 273 mm.
    Jellicoe and Kitchener, each 170 mm square. British.

19 Pincushion, 70 mm. British.
    Puzzle, 100 mm. British.
    China plate, 200 mm. British.

21 Sopwith Camel from commemorative brochure *Our Part in the Great War*, Ruston and Hornsby, Engineers, Lincoln.
    Popular print. I.W.M. Japanese.

22 'Fragments from France', p. 4. *The Bystander*,

London. British.

Crest dug-out, 88 mm. 'Carlton', W & R. Stoke-on-Trent. Reg. No 660613. British.

23 Three crest tanks, left to right, 146, 146, and 111 mm. All 'Arcadian', A & S. Stoke-on-Trent. Reg. Nos. all 858588. British.

Money-box, 205 mm. Patent 1918. British.

Photograph bottom right, I.W.M.

24 Medal. British Museum, London. German.

28 Poster. I.W.M. German.

29 From a postcard, I.W.M.

31 Rabbit, *Simplicissimus* April-September 1916, p. 260. German.

Lion, *Simplicissimus* April-September 1916, p. 81. German.

32 British soldier and Old Bill from postcards. British.

33 Poster. I.W.M. Australian.

'Scruffy Aussie' signed 'David Barker, Gallipoli, '15'. *The Anzac Book* Cassell & Co. Ltd, London, 1916, p. 22. Australian.

37 All I.W.M.

38/9 *La Baïonnette* Vol. XI pps. 40/41.

43 'Vive la France', 107 mm. 'Shelley' No. 406. British.

44 Walking-stick handle. I.W.M.

45 Ash-tray, 108 mm. Brass.

46 Crest monument, 163 mm. 'Carlton', W & R. Stoke-on-Trent. British.

47 *Lusitania* medal, 54 mm. Box, 80 mm. British replica of German original.

Iron crosses, frame 597 mm overall; largest medal, 70 mm. British.

48 *Simplicissimus* April-September 1916, p. 145. German.

52 *Pickelhaube*, 90 mm over sword. Silver plate with leather strap.

Crest steamroller, 123 mm. 'Arcadian', A & S. Stoke-on-Trent. British.

53 Bottom postcard, I.W.M. Italian.

56 Charms and mascots, I.W.M.

57 Bullet cross, 60 mm. Brass.

Bible and football from postcards.

58 Ref. from *Illustrierte Geschichte des Veldtkrieges*, 1914-16, Vol. IV p. 334. Union Deutsche Verlagsgesellschaft. German.

59 Reproduced from a postcard.

62 Tank, 400 mm over guns.

64 *Fragments from France* p. 35. British.

65 Postcards, French and German.

66 Inkwell, 172 mm. Spelter. French.

67 Top, largest gun, 290 mm. All brass.

Railway gun, 355 mm. Aluminium paint on metal.

Long gun, 335 mm.

Iron gun, 435 mm. German.

69 *Punch* 27 September 1916. British.

70/1 Largest tank, 400 mm; smallest, 40 mm.

72 Money-box, 390 mm.

73 Brass money-box, 240 mm.

Wood money-box, 250 mm.

Mad tank, 225 mm.

Soap tank, advertisement from back cover of *Fragments from France, No. Four.*

74 From *Canada in Khaki*, published for the Canadian War Records Office by The Pictorial Newspaper Co. (1910) Ltd., Bouverie Street, London.

75 Gas masks. I.W.M.

76 Dummy tree. Photograph: I.W.M.

Dummy horse, *The Great War in Gravure, New York Times War Portfolio.* United States.

Ref. from *Twenty Years After* p. 1189; Newnes. British.

Comic tree from *La Baïonnette.*

77 Reproduced from postcards.

79 Model ship, 545 mm.

80 HMS *Neptune*, 170 mm high.

81 Smallest figure, 50 mm; large figure, 190 mm. French.

82 Brass submarine, 100 mm.

83 Torpedo, 150 mm; Red Cross ships, 170 mm. Various makers; conical mine by W. H. Goss.

84 *Simplicissimus* April-September 1916, p. 160. German.

85 *Simplicissimus* April-September 1916, p. 93. German.

86 *Manchester Guardian History of the War* Vol. III p. 121, 1915.

89 Fretwork pattern, *Hobbies* July-December 1915, p. 643. Norfolk County Library. British.

91 Top, from an advertising postcard.

Bottom left, advertisement from *Simplicissimus*.

Aviator, 360 mm. Wooden cut-out. I.W.M. French.

92 Triplane, 130 mm wingspan. Nickel-plate on brass.

Parasol monoplane, 200 mm wingspan. Brass and aluminium.

Biplane, 117 mm wingspan. Brass.

94 Top left, 134 mm wingspan.

Top right, 114 mm long.

Middle, 174 mm wingspan.

Bottom, 434 mm long. Painted wood and metal.

95 Epergne, 330 mm wingspan. Mahogany.

96 L 33, 155 mm.

Airman, 140 mm. Various makers. British.

97 Tapemeasure, 900 mm. Brass and aluminium, blue linen tape.

Inkwell, 200 mm. Silver-plate and glass.

Zeppelin, 155 mm. Brass and steel. British.

98 Poster. I.W.M.

Baby from *Simplicissimus* April-September 1916, p. 83.

102 Parachutist, 560 mm. Silk and wool. British.

Triplane, 104 mm wingspan. Brass, painted.

Biplane, left, 76 mm wingspan. Brass.

Biplane, right, 70 mm wingspan. Copperplate on brass.

106 Biscuit-tin, 146 mm. Australian.

108 Periscope, 92 mm. Metal and glass. 'Copyright' by France 1914'.

109 Easter egg, 63 mm. China. Loaned by John and Venetia Newall. Russian.
Cigarette box, 130 mm. Brass. Upper one loaned by Mary Adshead. British, 1914.
112 Top, 111 mm.
Bottom, 1105 mm × 635 mm. Mercerized cotton on wool. Presumed Belgian.
114 'Blighty', 113 mm.
Pen-wiper, 110 mm. Painted wood and cloth.
117 Snake, 1945 mm. Turkish.
Box, 116 mm. Aluminium. British
120 Collecting-box, 444 mm. Painted wood. British.
Brooch, 27 mm. Metal. German.
122 Teapot, 222 mm. Food poster, 380 mm.
123 China whisky bottle, 245 mm. James Green & Nephew, London. Pat. No. 12748. 8 September 1916.
124 Inkwell, 360 mm. I.W.M.
Paper bag, 150 mm. Loaned by Mary Adshead. British.
126 *Poy's War Cartoons*, Simpkin, Marshall, Hamilton, Kent & Co. Ltd.
128 Top left, *La Baïonnette*, Vol. V, p. 216 by Gerda Wegener, 1916.
129 *La Baïonnette*, Vol. III, p. 195.
133 280 mm over frame. Water colour on card.
134 Ring box, 53 mm. British.
Purse, 48 mm. I.W.M. German.
137 Top right, munition worker, 140 mm. 'Carlton', Stoke-on-Trent. British.
140 Mould, 125 mm. Steel.
141 477 mm over figure. Painted by Samuel Finburgh. British, 1915. Reproduced by courtesy of the Victoria and Albert Museum, London.
142 Left, from a British photograph.
Right, statuette, 320 mm. Painted plaster. British.
145 Gun carriage, 105 mm overall. German.
Warship, 390 mm.
Tanks; largest 210 mm, smallest 120 mm. German.
146 Kaiser, 52 mm. British.
Bleriot monoplane, 59 mm wingspan. French.
Cut-outs; 55 mm average height. Printed paper on wood. French.
Machine gunner, 74 mm. French.
147 1 Standing figures, 30 mm. British.
2 Right-hand figure, 82 mm. British.
3, 4 & 5 Standing figures, 30 mm high approximately. German.
6 55 mm without rifle. French.
7 & 8 Infantry, 55 mm approximately. Swedish.
9 Standing figures, 25 mm. British.

149 Reproduced from postcards.
150 'We Shell' by Louis Wain.
Central Powers rabbit, postcard, I.W.M.
151 Tirpitz photograph, I.W.M.
Dog, 150 mm. I.W.M. Chinese.
156 Pile of German guns etc., ref: from French photograph.
Great Victory Exhibition, reproduced from a postcard.
158 Bottom: Vimy, from a Canadian photograph.
161 Tank monument, from a British photograph.
Arc de Triomphe, reproduced from a French postcard.
162 Lutyens drawing, reproduced by courtesy of the Royal Institute of British Architects Drawings Collection, London.
Cenotaph model reproduced from a postcard.
163 Crest memorials; tallest, 166 mm. Various makers.
Cenotaphs, left to right: 236 mm. Mahogany with brass plates. 155 mm. Wood, 200 mm. Brass. All British.
165 Memorial frame, 318 mm. Cast iron, painted. German.
166 Top: Pickelhaube, 118 mm. Copper and brass.
Gun inkwell, 191 mm. Gunmetal, bronze and aluminium 'Cast from metal ex-surrendered German Battleship *Helgoland*.' Thomas W. Ward Ltd, Sheffield, 1922. British.
Tank inkwell, 125 mm. Spelter. French.
Bottom: Centre back aeroplane, 178 mm wingspan.
Collectors' soldiers at right made by Hinton-Hunt and painted by Ken Kearsley, London. British.
168 Reproduced from a postcard.
169 *Fragments from France, No. Seven*, p. 31.
176 Memorial, 553 mm. Wood, brass, steel, copper and aluminium, part painted. British.

We have quoted from John Brophy and Eric Partridge *The Long Trail; The British Army 1914–18* Deutsch, rev. ed. 1965; Sphere Books, London, 1969.
For further information on the posters of the First World War we recommend:
Martin Hardie and Arthur K. Sabin *War Posters* A & C Black 1920.
M. Rickards (ed) *Posters of the First World War* Evelyn, 1968.
Joseph Darracott and Belinda Loftus *First World War Posters* Her Majesty's Stationery office, London 1972.

Index

Weapons and images of them are grouped under 'Technology of Warfare'. Other groupings include aircraft, cartoons, postcards etc. Subjects which have a chapter devoted to them (e.g. animals) are not indexed separately.

Page references in bold refer to illustrations.